TEEN TRAILBLAZERS

"BE THE CHANGE
YOU WISH TO SEE
IN THE WORLD."

–MOHANDAS GANDHI

TEEN TRAILBLAZERS

30 DARING BOYS
WHOSE DREAMS CHANGED THE WORLD

JENNIFER CALVERT

ILLUSTRATED BY
VESNA ASANOVIC

CASTLE POINT BOOKS
NEW YORK

Teen Trailblazers: 30 Daring Boys Whose Dreams Changed the World

Copyright © 2022 by St. Martin's Press.

All rights reserved. Printed in Singapore.

For information, address St. Martin's Publishing Group, 120 Broadway, New York, NY 10271.

www.castlepointbooks.com

The Castle Point Books trademark is owned by Castle Point Publishing, LLC.
Castle Point books are published and distributed by St. Martin's Publishing Group.

ISBN 978-1-250-28161-6 (trade paperback)
ISBN 978-1-250-28162-3 (ebook)

Design by Katie Jennings Campbell
Composition by Noora Cox

Our books may be purchased in bulk for promotional, educational, or business use.
Please contact your local bookseller or the Macmillan Corporate and Premium Sales
Department at 1-800-221-7945, extension 5442, or by email at
MacmillanSpecialMarkets@macmillan.com.

First Edition: 2022

10 9 8 7 6 5 4 3 2 1

CONTENTS

"IF YOU CAN'T FLY, THEN RUN,
IF YOU CAN'T RUN, THEN WALK,
IF YOU CAN'T WALK, THEN CRAWL,
BUT WHATEVER YOU DO, YOU HAVE
TO KEEP MOVING FORWARD."

—MARTIN LUTHER KING JR.

"ALL LIFE IS AN EXPERIMENT.
THE MORE EXPERIMENTS
YOU MAKE, THE BETTER."

—RALPH WALDO EMERSON

"A CHANGE IS BROUGHT ABOUT
BECAUSE ORDINARY PEOPLE DO
EXTRAORDINARY THINGS."

—PRESIDENT BARACK OBAMA

INTRODUCTION

Even *thinking* about changing the world can feel pretty intimidating. But remember this: every great scientist, activist, writer, and inventor started out exactly as you are today—a kid with a dream, a talent, a curious mind, and a desire to find their place in the world. Trailblazers are the ones who keep moving in the direction of their dreams, no matter what obstacles they face along the way, and they carve out a path for others to follow.

The men in this book were *teen* trailblazers not because they changed the world while they were young (although some did), but because that's when the seeds of change were planted and cultivated in each of them. Looking at their incredible legacies, we can see the seeds being sown by fate; nurtured by passion, curiosity, kindness, and even frustration; and blossoming into action, inspiration, and advocacy. These boys grew into the trailblazers they were meant to be, the trailblazers the world needed them to be.

Walt Disney's (page 43) love of drawing as a boy led him to create a media and entertainment empire that brings joy to millions. Satoshi Tajiri (page 99) turned his bug-collecting hobby into Pokémon, a game that inspired generations of collectors and gamers. Colin Kaepernick (page 111) not only fulfilled his childhood dream of taking an NFL team to the Superbowl but also created a movement to stand up against the discrimination he'd faced for just as long. The seeds of greatness were always there.

Although they have accomplished what feel like superhuman feats, these changemakers were, and are, all human, all flawed. And many of them would be quick to tell you that. Nelson Mandela (page 59) once said, "I am not a saint, unless you think of a saint as a sinner who just keeps on trying." They dealt with doubt, embraced prejudices, made mistakes, and suffered setbacks. But if you think about it, that's pretty comforting. It's proof that you don't have to be perfect to change the world. You just have to keep trying.

Wilbur and Orville Wright (page 27) kept trying to fly, even though the world said it was impossible. Frederick Douglass (page 23) kept trying to escape the bonds of slavery; he not only found his way to freedom but also became one of the most powerful voices against slavery in history. Tim Berners-Lee (page 87) is *still* trying to turn the World Wide Web into what he knows it can be, and he isn't going to stop until he succeeds.

These stories are just the beginning—the germination of ideas and adventures to come. There is so much more to learn about each of these incredible trailblazers and others like them. So, keep reading. Keep learning. And keep trying! You'll be amazed by the seeds already inside you, just waiting for a chance to bloom.

BENJAMIN BANNEKER

MATHEMATICIAN AND ASTRONOMER

BORN: 1731 · DIED: 1806

- One of the first Black men in America to gain distinction in science, publishing his findings in his own yearly almanac
- Spent 50 years observing and documenting the 17-year life cycle of the cicada

"PRESUMPTION SHOULD NEVER MAKE US NEGLECT THAT WHICH APPEARS EASY TO US, NOR DESPAIR MAKE US LOSE COURAGE AT THE SIGHT OF DIFFICULTIES." –BENJAMIN BANNEKER

Do you ever wonder what makes things tick? Or have you even taken things apart to find out? You're not alone. Some people are born with the kind of curious mind that makes them see everything as a puzzle to be solved. Benjamin Banneker was one of those people, and the constant hum of his clever brain helped him become an esteemed scientist, a respected political figure, and an early anti-slavery activist at a time of entrenched inequality in the United States.

Born free to grow up on his family's tobacco farm at a time when slavery wouldn't be abolished for another 130 years, Benjamin stood out from the beginning. As he grew older, he continued to make his mark on the world through scientific study and political activism, even publishing his findings and opinions so others could benefit from them. In fact, he was one of the first Black scientists to be published in the United States.

Benjamin's accomplishments are all the more impressive when you find out that he was mostly self-taught. It's not that Benjamin didn't go to school (he did), but his thirst for knowledge didn't end with the school day. He couldn't get enough of science, math, and astronomy. That curiosity led him to notice the odd habits of a funny, not-so-little insect called the cicada.

No one knew much about the behavior of cicadas at the time, but Benjamin sensed that there was something different about them. He first noticed them when he was a teenager, and he spent the next 50 years of his life observing their habits and predicting their next emergence. He has been credited as the first person to observe and document the 17-year life cycle of the cicada, which lives most of its life underground before emerging to spend a few noisy weeks aboveground.

The cicada life cycle wasn't the only natural phenomenon Benjamin kept an eye on. He also taught himself astronomy and predicted lunar and solar eclipses more accurately than well-known experts in the field. Benjamin packaged the information alongside helpful medical advice, tidal charts, and essays in the yearly almanacs he published. As an experienced beekeeper who made and sold his own mead (an alcoholic beverage made with fermented honey), he also published information on bees.

MAN OR MYTH

When you read more about Benjamin, you're sure to discover incredible stories of his many accomplishments. But some may be just that—stories. According to certain sources, Benjamin made the first wooden clock in America. Others state that he was appointed by President George Washington to plan the layout of Washington, DC. Some go even further to say that he had a photographic memory that helped him redraw the plans from scratch when Charles L'Enfant left the country with them in a huff. Benjamin did build a wooden clock by taking apart and studying a stopwatch. And he did assist in the planning of Washington, DC. Whether or not the other stories are true, Benjamin's documented accomplishments are more than enough to make him a trailblazer.

Although Benjamin's almanacs were well respected for their scientific insights, it was the political content that many people found most interesting. In addition to opinion pieces, Benjamin included his correspondence with Founder and future president Thomas Jefferson. Thomas was the person who wrote "all men are created equal" into the U.S. Constitution, and he was a vocal opponent of slavery. He also enslaved more than 600 people in his lifetime. Seeing that conflict, Benjamin set out to convince Thomas to fight to abolish slavery for good.

In an eloquent and respectful letter, Benjamin pointed out the hypocrisy of Revolutionary leaders enslaving people of color while fighting the British for their own independence. He also included a recent copy of his scholarly almanac as proof that a Black man like himself was indeed (and at least) equal to any white man. Thomas responded to the letter immediately, thanking Benjamin for the almanac and admitting that it was proof that people of color deserved better opportunities than prejudice and slavery afforded them. But he fell

USE YOUR VOICE

There's an old saying (the author of which is unknown) that goes, "The only thing necessary for the triumph of evil is for good men to do nothing." Benjamin wasn't enslaved; he didn't need to fight for his own freedom. He could have kept quiet about the injustices of slavery and made his own life easier. But as a free Black man with political connections, Benjamin was in a unique position to create change. He used his privilege to speak out against those injustices and to challenge the people benefiting from them. In doing so, he gave a voice to those who couldn't use theirs, those who might have been punished or even killed for speaking up.

short of agreeing to any sort of political action and later belittled Benjamin in a letter to a friend.

Benjamin wasn't deterred. He published both his own letter and Thomas's in the next almanac, which flew off the shelves and ignited a renewed conversation about slavery. After that, Benjamin let his almanacs and his lifetime of scientific study do the talking for him. Benjamin truly was one of a kind, offering contribution after contribution to a society that treated people of color like their only value was in forced labor. His curious mind set others spinning!

WOLFGANG AMADEUS MOZART

MUSICAL COMPOSER

BORN: 1756 · DIED: 1791

- Started playing music professionally when he was just 6 years old
- Shaped the nature of classical music through more than 100 original pieces

"LOVE, LOVE, LOVE— THAT IS THE SOUL OF GENIUS."

—WOLFGANG MOZART

Few words in the English language inspire as much annoyance as the word "practice." Everything we do in life takes practice—playing music, doing math, having patience, kicking a soccer ball. There's no escaping it. Not one person became a trailblazer without practicing. Not even musical genius Wolfgang Amadeus Mozart. In fact, he practiced more than most.

Talented composer Leopold Mozart was teaching his daughter, Maria Anna, how to play the harpsichord when he noticed his son, Wolfgang, mimicking the movements of her fingers. Wolfgang was just 3 years old, but his dad let him join in on his sister's lessons. When Leopold discovered his son's incredible talent for music, he devoted himself to teaching him. The lessons were fun, but they weren't easy—Leopold insisted on perfection. Still, Wolfgang excelled, writing his first composition when he was just 5 years old.

Seeing that Wolfgang had outgrown his lessons, Leopold recognized an opportunity:

people would pay good money to see child prodigies perform. He started carting his children all over Europe to give concerts for wealthy, upper-class audiences. The tours took a toll on the family's health, though, and they often had to postpone or cancel performances due to illness. But Wolfgang got to meet and learn from other famous composers on the road, which helped him develop his own composition style.

The types of music Wolfgang made depended on his influences at the time. When he was 13 years old, he and his father left on the first of several trips to Italy. Something about the country inspired Wolfgang to write three operas while visiting: *Mitridate, re di Ponto* (1769), *Ascanio in Alba* (1771), and *Lucio Silla* (1772). When the pair came home, Wolfgang became an assistant concertmaster and wrote his only five violin concertos. By 1776, he was more interested in the piano, writing a number of pieces for it, including the Piano Concerto Number 9 in E flat major.

PRACTICE MAKES PRODIGIES

Wolfgang was considered a prodigy—someone who's naturally gifted and exceptional at something. But he wasn't born writing complex sonatas. Many experts today believe that prodigies are the result of a combination of three things: good genetics (they inherit their talent from a family member), opportunity to learn, and lots and lots of hard work. If Wolfgang's dad hadn't been a composer, taught him how to play, *and* made him practice, Wolfgang might never have become a composer himself. But the fact that he embraced his talent, fell in love with composing, and continued to work hard at it is why he's the history-making musician we know today.

Like many geniuses do, Wolfgang eventually got bored with his work. He felt he could do more if only he could leave his hometown of Salzburg, Austria, for bigger cities. With his sister as his companion, Wolfgang traveled to Mannheim, Paris, and Munich in search of more interesting and profitable work. But he returned home, unemployed and out of money, when his mother died in 1778.

"IF ONLY THE WORLD COULD FEEL THE POWER OF HARMONY." —WOLFGANG MOZART

Wolfgang took a job as a court organist and began producing pieces of church music, including his famous Coronation Mass. But in 1781, a run-in with a rude archbishop caused him to uproot his life. Archbishop von Colloredo summoned Wolfgang to Vienna, only to treat him like a servant instead of a world-class musician. Wolfgang angrily resigned his post, but he decided to give Vienna a try on his own.

Wolfgang flourished in the city, taking on students, writing music, and giving concerts. He met famous musicians like Johann Sebastian Bach and George Frideric Handel, who would come to influence his later work. He also met his wife in Vienna and started a family of his own. Thanks to Wolfgang's success, they enjoyed a happy life there.

Unfortunately, Wolfgang had a bad habit of overspending, and his work slowly dried up. The musical visionary spent many of the last years of his short life borrowing money from friends and family to cover his bills. But he never stopped creating, and he produced some of his best work in those years.

Thanks to his relentless devotion to music, Wolfgang was able to secure a good future for his wife, who published his works and organized memorial concerts in his honor. He also secured the future of classical music by influencing future generations and helping to make symphony, opera, string ensemble, and concerto what they are today. We may have Wolfgang's dad to thank for making the young musician practice, but Wolfgang's passion is what made him a trailblazing composer.

WHAT COULD HAVE BEEN

As a woman, Wolfgang Mozart's sister Maria Anna was expected to stop performing in public when she was old enough to marry. At the time, society felt that it was unladylike for females to pursue a career in the spotlight—or any career at all. So, by the time she was 18, Maria Anna had stopped performing with her brother. If Maria Anna had been allowed to continue performing, who knows what she might have accomplished! These gifted siblings might have taken the world by storm together.

ALEXANDER HAMILTON

FOUNDER

BORN: 1755 · DIED: 1804

- Wrote the papers that helped convince delegates to ratify the U.S. Constitution
- Built the financial foundation of the nation as the first secretary of the U.S. Treasury

"ALL THE GENIUS I HAVE LIES IN THIS; WHEN I HAVE A SUBJECT IN HAND, I STUDY IT PROFOUNDLY." —ALEXANDER HAMILTON

Alexander Hamilton's story sounds like something out of a Harry Potter book. Abandoned by his father, orphaned when his mother died, and passed to family members who died shortly thereafter, Alexander was plagued by tragedy as a child. He might not have had magic, but he did have courage and cleverness, and he knew he had to make his own way in the world. At the age of 11 (and with no Hogwarts to head to), Alexander took a job as a clerk at a trading company.

At 15 years old, Alexander's hunger for knowledge and success earned him a kind of scholarship—several people he impressed at home in St. Croix raised enough money to send him to school in America. He arrived in 1772, just before the war with Great Britain over American independence. Alexander couldn't help but get involved. While attending King's College in New York, he started writing brochures and speaking at rallies in support of the colonies' cause. And when the

THE FEDERALIST PAPERS

A COLLECTION OF ESSAYS IN FAVOR OF THE NEW CONSTITUTION

HAMILTON, MADISON & JAY

Revolutionary War broke out in 1775, he quit school to join the Continental Army.

Alexander was a fearless soldier, but he was an even more impressive leader. His clever mind hummed with military strategies and inspiring calls to action alike. Alexander

knew what the soldiers needed physically and emotionally, and he longed to lead them in battle. The Commander in Chief of the Continental Army (and future first president of the United States), George Washington, had other plans for him. Seeing Alexander's brilliant mind as an asset, George asked him to help manage things from the sidelines. Alexander served as Washington's assistant for 4 years. In that time, he watched how the newly formed United States was being run, and he wasn't happy about it.

Alexander believed that the country would be more powerful if the individual states worked together as one. So, when it came time to write the U.S. Constitution, he made the argument for giving more power to the federal government. Representatives from the states weren't on board with giving up the control they felt they'd just earned from the British. But Alexander wrote 51 of 85 persuasive essays, collectively called *The Federalist*

BRAVERY ON THE BATTLEFIELD

Alexander was sensitive about his humble beginnings and felt that he had to work even harder to prove himself. In his mind, being triumphant on the battlefield was his best chance. So, when George Washington chose someone else to lead the assault on Redoubt 10 in what would be the last major land battle of the war, Alexander fought for the position and got it. He then designed the brilliant strategy of silently surrounding the enemy at night and forcing them to surrender, which prevented countless injuries and deaths. He even made his men empty their guns so none could go off accidentally and give them away. His plan worked perfectly: he won the battle and made a name for himself in the process. Alexander made sure not to toot his own horn, though (which might have lost him the recently earned respect of his peers). When he wrote about the battle, he gave all the credit to his men.

Papers, convincing them to go along with the plan. Thanks to Alexander's efforts, the U.S. Constitution was ratified (signed and put into practice) by the next year.

When George Washington won the presidency in 1789, he wanted Alexander by his side again. He appointed Alexander as the first secretary of the Treasury (a.k.a. the head of the department that's responsible for the country's money). Alexander's mind whirred to life again, tackling all the problems the new country was about to face and coming up with solutions.

Other countries had loaned the Revolutionaries money to fight the war against England, and it was time to pay up. Alexander established the systems that made that possible. He also created the first national bank (aptly named First Bank of the United States) to handle the government's financial business.

Sadly, Alexander was killed at the age of 49 in a famous duel with fellow politician Aaron Burr. But his work and legacy as a Founder of the United States have outlived

A COMPLICATED HISTORY

Alexander grew up in the Caribbean, where the British had established several colonies to grow crops like sugarcane. It wasn't the British who were working the fields, however—they brought enslaved people over from Africa to do their planting and harvesting. Having seen firsthand the cruelty the enslaved people experienced, Alexander became an outspoken opponent of slavery. He even tried to pass several laws to bring an end to it. But he was also a product of his time, and it's been discovered that he, too, kept slaves. No one knows why he both benefited from slavery and railed against it, or how he treated his own slaves. One can only guess that he was ready to move on from the practice and to bring the country with him.

him by 200 years—something the ambitious 11-year-old version of him would have been thrilled to know. Despite his unhappy upbringing, Alexander helped the United States of America work through its own early growing pains to become the nation we know today.

"THOSE WHO STAND FOR NOTHING FALL FOR ANYTHING."

—ALEXANDER HAMILTON

RALPH WALDO EMERSON

ESSAYIST AND PHILOSOPHER

BORN: 1803 · DIED: 1882

- One of the most influential writers and philosophers in American history
- Led the transcendentalist movement, which defined a generation

"OUR GREATEST GLORY IN LIFE IS NOT IN NEVER FAILING, BUT IN RISING UP EVERY TIME WE FAIL."

—RALPH WALDO EMERSON

It's easy to think that a philosopher isn't as influential as an explorer or a leader. But what do protests, scientific discoveries, art, invention, and philosophy all have in common? They all begin with an idea. And that's great news, because it means that absolutely anyone can change the world.

Simply by sharing his thoughts, Ralph Waldo Emerson—or Waldo, as he liked to be called—created a movement that educated, inspired, and influenced great minds for generations after him. He

SO, WHAT IS IT?

Transcendentalism is a big word for a simple idea: that people should follow their own hearts and imaginations. Or as Waldo put it, "Trust thyself." He believed that everyone had the power to look inside themselves and to find everything they need, and that outside influences (like religion or society) just get in the way. He wanted people to think for themselves.

traveled the world, rubbed elbows with the greatest thinkers of his time, and wrote essays that still have the power to change perspectives more than a century later. Some might say it was all thanks to natural intellect (he did start at Harvard when he was just 14 years old). But more than anything, Waldo changed the world simply by being excited about new ideas.

Waldo didn't just attend Harvard, either. In the summer, he also taught and waited tables. He and one of his brothers even

wrote papers for other students to help make ends meet—a job that could have gotten him expelled from school. When Waldo graduated, he taught at his brother's school for a few years before heading back to Cambridge to attend the Divinity School at Harvard to become a Unitarian minister.

A GREAT AUNT

Waldo was a fairly progressive thinker for the era, including being a supporter of women's rights. But that should be no surprise—he grew up surrounded by strong, intelligent women. When Waldo's father died just before he turned 8 years old, it was his mom and his aunts who raised him and his siblings. Waldo's aunt Mary Moody Emerson, in particular, was a brilliant woman who taught him the importance of reading. She also encouraged Waldo and his brothers to think for themselves. When they were growing up, Mary insisted that the boys form an opinion on every important topic of the day. Her thirst for knowledge and independent spirit inspired a lot of Waldo's later philosophies.

After the death of his first wife in 1831, Waldo started to have doubts about the church. He felt that organized religion was outdated, and that there were better ways to worship. The next year, he left the ministry and traveled to Europe, where he met some of the great minds of his time. In the company of William Wordsworth, Samuel Taylor Coleridge, John Stuart Mill, and Thomas Carlyle, Waldo started to form some of his philosophies. He also had a revelation on a visit to the Jardin des Plantes, a famous botanical garden in Paris. In viewing all of the gardens' plants organized by classification, he saw a larger connection between nature and the divine. It was a turning point that would lead him to his life's purpose.

No longer working as a pastor but still needing to make a living, Waldo began touring as a lecturer and sharing some of the ideas he'd been cultivating during his travels. His ideas weren't always popular, but they started to shake things up and to make people think a little differently. He wrote some of his ideas down in his first essay, *Nature*, which he self-published in 1836.

Around the same time, he gathered a group of like-minded scholars to form the Transcendental Club. This was the beginning of a movement—just a group of friends talking about new ideas. Together with fellow member Margaret Fuller, Waldo founded a magazine called *The Dial* and published some of the best musings of the day. He also published two collections of his own essays—named *Essays: First Series* and *Essays: Second Series*—that would earn him a reputation as a philosopher and push transcendentalism into the spotlight.

Waldo spent the rest of his life writing and giving lectures. Never one to shy away from controversy, he became an outspoken abolitionist, and his speeches called for an end to slavery. He was also lucky enough to meet with President Abraham Lincoln on the subject before the president's death. But Waldo's controversial opinions weren't his only legacy. His ideas influenced other great writers and thinkers, like Henry

THE EVOLUTION OF WALDO

Although he graduated from college in the middle of his class, Waldo read everything he could get his hands on. He actually read so much that it started to affect his eyesight! But all that reading also expanded his mind and helped him to see religion from a different perspective. Although he served as a pastor on and off for several years, he later argued that organized religion gets in the way of a true connection to God. Divinity and knowledge, he believed, were already inside each of us.

David Thoreau, Walt Whitman, and Friedrich Nietzsche, not to mention the students studying them today. And the transcendentalist movement went on to impact not just literature and education but also architecture, politics, current events, and art. So, whether you think your ideas might make a great splash or cause quiet ripples, share them. One idea could change everything.

LOUIS BRAILLE

INVENTOR

BORN: 1809 · DIED: 1852

- Invented the braille code, which gives people who are visually impaired a means of written communication
- Fought for the fair treatment of people with visual impairment

"BRAILLE IS KNOWLEDGE, AND KNOWLEDGE IS POWER."

–LOUIS BRAILLE

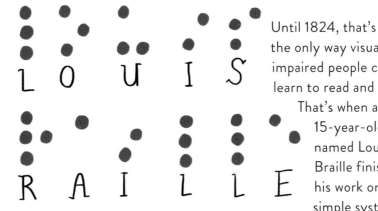

Can you remember how hard it was to learn to read and write? Think about how many times you had to practice each letter before you could write a word. Imagine that you've never actually seen any writing—not a single letter, let alone a full page of words—and you have to learn by running your fingers over raised letters and memorizing each shape. Now imagine that you can't see what you're writing or the paper you're writing it on, and you can't read anything you've written. How much harder would that be?

Until 1824, that's the only way visually impaired people could learn to read and write. That's when a 15-year-old boy named Louis Braille finished his work on a simple system of raised dots that would change the lives of millions of visually impaired people—people like him. Roughly 200 years later, the braille system is still helping people with visual impairments communicate.

Louis lost his sight slowly and painfully after an accident in his father's leather workshop. While he was "helping" his dad punch holes in a piece of leather, the tool (called an awl) bounced and hit the precocious 3-year-old in his eye. Despite an immediate visit to the doctor, the eye became infected. Over the next 2 years, the infection spread to Louis's other eye and blinded him.

Luckily for Louis, his parents were incredibly supportive and helped him have a full and happy childhood. He found his way around his village and attended a local school using a cane his father made

for him. Not only was he smart, but he was also a talented musician. He became a respected cellist and organist, going on to play the organ for several Catholic churches in France.

Louis was incredibly bright—bright enough to win a scholarship to the National Institute for Blind Youth in Paris at the age of 10—but he didn't create his system from thin air. He built it on a concept created by Charles Barbier. Charles believed that learning to write was too hard for most people and almost impossible for those who were visually impaired. To make it simpler, he created a system of grids, symbols, and tools that allowed the reader to read and write by touch.

A REAL UNDERSTANDING

They say that necessity is the mother of invention, which means that we often come up with solutions only when we're faced with a problem. That was certainly true for Louis. Although Charles Barbier's system was good, Charles couldn't truly understand the needs of a visually impaired person because he wasn't one. Louis's firsthand knowledge helped fill some of its gaps, proving that you need to fully understand the problem in order to come up with the right solution.

Charles's system used different combinations of 12 punched holes (ironically, punched by the same tool that blinded Louis) to represent different sounds. It allowed students to take notes and reread what they'd written, which was entirely new for the visually impaired community. But without punctuation, capitalization, or numbers, his methods were still pretty confusing.

Once he'd learned Charles's system at school, Louis spent every waking hour outside of class trying to improve it. The task took 3 years, but the new system was both easier to understand and more flexible. It used combinations of just 6 raised dots to represent each of 64 letters, punctuation marks, sounds, signs, numbers, and conjunctions.

Louis didn't just want to create a way for visually impaired people to read and write. He wanted to create a way for them to *learn*. Having access to communication and knowledge, he argued, was crucial if visually impaired people were ever to be treated as equal to people with full sight. His system created an equal footing. Louis had grown up learning only what he could listen to, and that meant missing out on a whole world of knowledge. He wanted more for others like him.

That's why, after finishing school, Louis stayed on at the National Institute for Blind Youth as a teacher. The school was happy to employ him, but they refused to employ his methods.

BEAUTIFUL MUSIC

As a musician, Louis had a keen interest in being able to read and write music for himself, so he created a way to translate sheet music into braille. Louis assigned each note a braille letter, which was placed at the top of a dotted cell. The bottom two dots were used to indicate the note's length. And everything else the musician needs to know—rhythm, pitch, and other directions—was placed before the first cell. Learning to read music this way can be tricky, especially because it's based on Louis's native French, but it gave visually impaired people the ability to enjoy music the same way that sighted people do.

One headmaster was even fired from his job for translating a history book into braille. But the Institute's students demanded that braille become the school's official writing system. Louis had died just 2 years earlier.

Thanks to an abundance of technology that reads and writes text for those with visual impairments, braille is used less frequently today. But the braille system continues to make communication and everyday life more accessible for millions of people. Louis would surely be thrilled that those in need have better resources than he could ever have imagined.

FREDERICK DOUGLASS

AUTHOR AND ABOLITIONIST

BORN: 1818 · DIED: 1895

- Former enslaved person who became one of the leaders of the abolition movement
- Wrote five memoirs about his experiences, giving a voice to enslaved people

"I PREFER TO BE TRUE TO MYSELF, EVEN AT THE HAZARD OF INCURRING THE RIDICULE OF OTHERS, RATHER THAN TO BE FALSE, AND TO INCUR MY OWN ABHORRENCE." —FREDERICK DOUGLASS

Frederick Bailey (later Frederick Douglass)—one of the greatest writers in American history—was born sometime around 1818. You might be thinking, "Why don't we know when he was born?" The truth is, not even Frederick himself knew. He was born into slavery, and enslaved people were given as little information as possible as a rule. Frederick would spend his whole life fighting for that to change, for enslaved people to have access to knowledge, freedom, and human rights.

Being born into slavery meant Frederick had absolutely no control over his own life. To enslavers, people of color like

BORN INTO SLAVERY

Frederick never knew who his father was; he only knew that his father was white. Historians have guessed that his father might have been his mother's enslaver, Captain Anthony, or one of that man's family members. Because enslavers felt entitled to the bodies of enslaved people, rape was not uncommon. And it didn't matter to them that the resulting children were their own flesh and blood. To them, the birth of a child to an enslaved mother meant just one thing: more slave labor.

Frederick were considered property, no different from the machinery or horses that served the plantation where he was born. Frederick was taken from his mother, Harriet Bailey, as a baby and was sent to live with his grandmother until he was old enough to work. That day came when he was just 6 or 7 years old. Frederick had no bed to sleep in, no cover when it got cold, and far too little food for a growing boy. But he was expected to corral the cows, feed the chickens, and do the bidding of his "master," Captain Anthony. Any enslaved person who didn't was badly beaten.

Not long after his arrival at Great House Farm, Frederick was handed off to work for a relative, Hugh Auld, in Baltimore. Hugh's wife, Sophia, was kind at first. She started teaching Frederick the alphabet, just as she taught her young son. Frederick was clever and quick to learn, but Hugh was furious with Sophia. Learning to read and write, he said, would make a person "unfit" for slavery. Hearing that changed Frederick's life. It was the moment he realized that education could be his ticket out of slavery.

Frederick found others to teach him, and he read everything he could get his hands on. The more he read, the angrier he became. White enslavers acted like slavery was natural, or even *moral*. They considered it their right and responsibility as members of the "superior race." But Frederick began to understand how hard they worked to preserve that lie. They tore babies from their mothers so they wouldn't have a sense of history, support, or belonging. They used whips and chains to keep enslaved people in check. And, most importantly to Frederick, they kept enslaved people from becoming educated. In other words, they did everything they could to keep the power dynamic the way they wanted it, because they knew slavery *wasn't* natural. And they knew that if enslaved people chose to rise up against them, they would lose everything.

Realizing this, Frederick started to fight back and to plan his escape. In response, he was sent to work for Edward Covey, a notorious "slave breaker." And break Frederick he did—in mind, body, and spirit. Edward worked Frederick to the bone and beat him so often and so badly that he lost all hope of escaping. But something in Frederick wasn't ready to give up. One day, he fought back for 2 long hours and won. Edward was so rattled that he didn't dare lay a hand on Frederick again.

It took a few failed escape attempts and a bit of jail time, but Frederick finally found his way north to New York City. He married his love, Anna Murray, and they continued on to Massachusetts together. But Frederick still wasn't a free man. He changed his last name to Douglass to help him hide from slave catchers.

Frederick couldn't hide for long, though. As he got more involved with the anti-slavery movement, his education and eloquence caught the attention of its leaders. Frederick was asked to give speeches about his experience, which led to his publishing his now-famous autobiography. He toured the country, writing more books and starting an anti-slavery newsletter called *The North Star.*

EQUAL RIGHTS FOR *EVERYONE*

Frederick didn't just want equal treatment for people of color, he wanted equal treatment for everyone. That included women at a time when they had few rights and little respect. After attending the First Women's Rights Convention in 1848, he made an impassioned argument for women to have the right to vote. He wrote, "All that distinguishes man as an intelligent and accountable being, is equally true of woman," and he went on to say that the United States government couldn't claim to be "for the people" if it kept women from having a say.

Soon, Frederick's fans raised enough money to buy his freedom.

With every word he spoke and wrote, Frederick changed hearts and minds on the subject of slavery. He helped people see the truth about it and the human cost of it. He's remembered today as one of the strongest voices in the abolition (anti-slavery) movement. And although no one knows his birthday, millions celebrate his life.

WILBUR & ORVILLE WRIGHT

INVENTORS

BORN: 1867, 1871 · DIED: 1912, 1948

- Invented not only the airplane but also the art of aviation
- Revolutionized travel and made it possible to go anywhere in the world

"IT IS POSSIBLE TO FLY WITHOUT MOTORS, BUT NOT WITHOUT KNOWLEDGE AND SKILL." —WILBUR WRIGHT

When Wilbur and Orville Wright were born in the mid-1800s, everyone knew a universal truth: human beings could not fly. It was impossible. But as Nelson Mandela (page 59) himself once said, "It always seems impossible until it's done." Thanks to the ingenuity of the Wright brothers, who believed the impossible was possible, an average of 6 million people now fly all over the world every day.

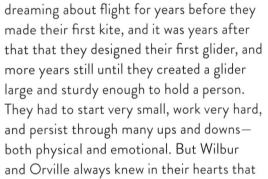

One thing that really might be impossible? Changing the world overnight. (But you never know!) The brothers had been dreaming about flight for years before they made their first kite, and it was years after that that they designed their first glider, and more years still until they created a glider large and sturdy enough to hold a person. They had to start very small, work very hard, and persist through many ups and downs—both physical and emotional. But Wilbur and Orville always knew in their hearts that human flight was possible, and that kept them going.

The boys were lucky to grow up with parents who prized learning and curiosity. They had plenty of toys to tinker with and books to read, and they had their parents' full permission

"IF WE ALL WORKED ON THE ASSUMPTION THAT WHAT IS ACCEPTED AS TRUE IS REALLY TRUE, THERE WOULD BE LITTLE HOPE OF ADVANCE."

—ORVILLE WRIGHT

to stay home from school when they were hard at work on projects of their own. They even credited their dad with first sparking their fascination with flight.

When Wilbur and Orville were very young, their father brought home with him a little toy helicopter. This wasn't the kind of helicopter that is used today by reporters and rescuers. This was a little whirligig made of a stick topped by a propeller and powered by twisting rubber bands. The simple toy set the boys' imaginations on fire, and they began dreaming of the day they would fly.

THE FAMILY BUSINESS

Wilbur and Orville's dad wasn't the only member of the family to encourage their endeavors. They inherited their mechanical abilities from their mom, Susan. She could make absolutely anything, they said. Susan had learned how to build things from her father, a carriage maker, and she often made toys for her children. She enjoyed watching her sons tinker and did everything she could to support their interests—even when it involved their making a mess in the house.

While their minds worked, so did their hands. Orville built and sold kites, and then he built a printing press that allowed the pair to publish newspapers. In the years after school, the brothers started the Wright Cycle Co., a business where they built and sold bicycles. But the business was mostly a way to fund their longtime dream. They started building their gliders right there in the shop.

In 1900, the brothers left for the beaches of Kitty Hawk, North Carolina, to take advantage of strong winds and soft dunes. They started out launching gliders, which usually crashed. Next, they built a biplane (a plane with one wing above another) with an ultralight engine. Although both brothers took turns manning the planes, the first successful flight took off with Orville at the helm and Wilbur running alongside. The plane flew for 12 seconds and traveled only 120 feet, but the brothers knew instantly that their idea had wings.

The brothers continued experimenting with larger planes and engines, developing controls still used today, and teaching themselves not only how to fly but also how to take off, land, and do loop-the-loops. While they were having fun and making history, the U.S. government was busy trying to make their own flying machines—and failing. The brothers wrote to Washington to offer up their invention, only to be turned away. Other countries, however, welcomed the Wrights' creation with open arms.

The brothers were invited to fly their plane in front of excited crowds in France. (Back then, the trip across the Atlantic took several weeks by boat. Today, thanks to the Wright brothers, it takes less than 12 hours.) Other countries soon followed suit, and the Wright brothers quickly became world famous for their creation.

After the Wrights' warm reception in Europe, the U.S. government finally took notice of the brothers' success and signed a contract with them. And it's a good thing, too—airplanes were essential to winning both World Wars. Today, airplanes do more than just get passengers from point A to point B. They also transport patients and medicine to hospitals, food and supplies to those in need, military equipment to troops, water to raging wildfires, and mail all over the world. We take these things for granted, but it wasn't all that long ago that the idea of such feats was considered preposterous. All it takes to change history is one person (or two!) saying it's possible.

THE WRIGHT SISTER

The brothers couldn't have done the impossible without their little sister, Katharine (Katie), by their side. She helped them get their ideas off the ground, ran the bicycle shop while they were experimenting on the sandy shores of North Carolina, and nursed Orville back to health after a terrible crash. She even helped negotiate her brothers' contract with the U.S. Signal Corps and learned French so that she could help them during their European tours. All in all, the Wrights were one impressive bunch!

MOHANDAS GANDHI

POLITICAL AND SPIRITUAL LEADER

BORN: 1869 · DIED: 1948

- Led the nonviolent revolution for India's independence from the British Empire
- Developed the methods of civil disobedience that would inspire leaders like Martin Luther King Jr.

"IN A GENTLE WAY, YOU CAN SHAKE THE WORLD."

—MOHANDAS GANDHI

What does it take to create change, stop injustice, and end wars? Mohandas Gandhi would tell you that all it takes is the desire to do so. He shook the world not with raised fists and voices, but with forgiveness, compassion, and hope for a better future. And in doing so, he became the Mahatma (which translates to "great soul")—an inspiration to generations of trailblazers who came after him.

Growing up in a well-respected and traditional family, Mohandas had some big expectations to live up to. His dad worked in government, and he encouraged Mohandas to do the same. For Mohandas, that meant going to law school in London, a city that was pretty strange and intimidating for a shy Hindu teen from India. At first, he spent lots of time and money trying to fit in. But it wasn't long before Mohandas did what he'd always done—he listened to his gut. He decided it was better to stay true to himself, to live simply, and to focus on his studies.

That decision helped Mohandas get through school and come to love both the law and London.

PEACEFUL FROM THE START

Mohandas was the baby of the family—the last of six children—and sometimes he acted like it. When his older brothers picked on him while they played outside, Mohandas would run home and tell his mom. But he often got a response he didn't understand: She'd ask him why he didn't just stick up for himself and hit back. Mohandas couldn't imagine hitting his brothers, or anyone else for that matter. He may have been a tattletale, but he was a nonviolent one.

But it didn't help him find his footing in the courtroom. While he was arguing his first case, his nerves got the better of him and his mind went completely blank. Mohandas quickly ran out of the room (but not before reimbursing his confused client). Soon after that, he took a year-long job in the South African state of Natal.

The cultural differences in London were small compared to those in South Africa. Like India, Natal was under British rule. But Mohandas was shocked by the government-endorsed racism and the injustice Indian immigrants faced there. With his upper-class upbringing, he had been spared the worst of the mistreatment dealt to lower castes in India. That was about to change.

Mohandas was sitting in the first-class compartment of the train, enjoying an ordinary day, when a white passenger complained about him being there. Mohandas was told to move to the back of the train, despite his having paid for a first-class ticket. When he refused, he was thrown off the train entirely. That night, he vowed to do whatever it took to fight against discrimination and the laws that allowed it.

Mohandas soon found his voice in his fight for justice, but he never raised it. Instead, he developed a method of resistance called *satyagraha*, or "devotion to truth," where he let his nonviolent actions speak for him. After taking up several causes in South Africa and making some headway there, Mohandas returned to India and began advocating for his home country's independence. He encouraged Indians to join peaceful protests, to boycott British goods, to leave British jobs, to stop attending British schools, and to respectfully ignore certain British laws in a movement he called "Quit India."

In 1930, Mohandas led a great protest against a hefty and decades-long tax on salt, which Indians used regularly but were forbidden by law to obtain for themselves. He and dozens of others marched 241 miles over 24 days to collect salt from evaporated seawater. Nearly 60,000 people, including Mohandas, were arrested along the way and in the following weeks as similar protests began sweeping across India. The salt tax stuck, but Indian citizens nearest the sea were finally allowed to collect their own salt, and Mohandas made a name for himself as Mahatma Gandhi, an Indian leader.

As Mohandas and his supporters continued their fight, they were jailed and freed, were brought to standstills, and forged compromises. But, in the end, they won, helping India gain independence from the British Empire in 1947. Sadly, Mohandas was assassinated just a year later. But his life and his method of satyagraha—now commonly known as civil disobedience—inspired leaders to come, including Martin Luther King Jr. (page 75), during the civil rights movement in the United States and Nelson Mandela (page 59) in ending government-sanctioned discrimination in South Africa. The shy, quiet boy from Porbandar, India, had become an unstoppable force for good and changed the world, all while staying true to himself.

UNTOUCHABLE

Although being evicted from the train was what inspired Mohandas's political career, he had been fighting against injustice his whole life. Young Mohandas didn't make friends easily—he preferred the company of his books—but he showed kindness to all. That included a boy his age named Uka who came to clean at his house. According to the Hindu caste system (a system that places some people above others and determines how they live), Uka was an Untouchable, the very lowest caste. Mohandas's mom warned him that touching someone like Uka was a sin, but Mohandas told his mom she was wrong. In his eyes, he and Uka were the same. Mohandas would later start a movement to make the Untouchable caste a thing of the past.

ERNEST SHACKLETON

ARCTIC EXPLORER

BORN: 1874 · DIED: 1922

- Achieved the rank of first mate in the Merchant Navy at the age of 18, becoming a certified master mariner 6 years later
- After a shipwreck in Antarctica, upheld leadership for 2 years, saving all 28 crewmembers

"I HAVE OFTEN MARVELED AT THE THIN LINE THAT SEPARATES SUCCESS FROM FAILURE." –ERNEST SHACKLETON

The ancient Greek philosopher Epictetus once wrote, "It's not what happens to you, but how you react to it that matters." Explorer Ernest Shackleton learned that lesson the hard way when, with its destination tantalizingly close, his ship hit thick, unmovable ice. The outlook for Ernest and the 28 other men on that ship was bleak, but his reaction proved to be the difference between life and death.

By most measurements, Ernest's expedition was a complete failure—his ship never even made it to Antarctica. The explorers spent an excruciating year cooped up in a ship with dozens of dogs and one misgendered tomcat named Mrs. Chippy, and another year fighting their way home. But thanks to Ernest's good sense, leadership, and ability to think on his feet, they persevered. And most people would say that bringing 28 men home alive when faced with stranding, starvation, frostbite, scurvy (a devastating vitamin deficiency), and short tempers is an even more impressive accomplishment than a successful expedition.

Ernest wasn't the first person to try to make the trek to Antarctica and back. Other men had succeeded, and still others had died trying. But Ernest didn't just want to set foot on Antarctica, he wanted to lead the first team to walk across the entire continent. And by August of 1914, he was ready and raring to go on a ship called the *Endurance*. That impatience to make history cost him dearly.

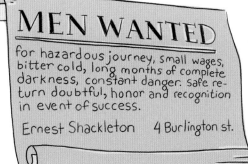

MEN WANTED

for hazardous journey, small wages, bitter cold, long months of complete darkness, constant danger, safe return doubtful, honor and recognition in event of success.

Ernest Shackleton   4 Burlington st.

The first obstacle the crew faced wasn't bad luck. It was bad judgment. Local sailors had warned Ernest against leaving with the ice so thick—so thick, in fact, it could stop a ship dead in the water. But Ernest didn't listen and, with the continent in sight, the ship came to a sudden halt. The time was January 1915, and Ernest knew he and his crew would have to camp out on the ship until the ice thawed enough for it to move.

That's when Ernest's survival skills kicked in, because the ice wasn't the only thing that could cause trouble for a group of stir-crazy explorers. The crew was pretty angry at being trapped together with little food and no guarantee of survival. Ernest forced them to follow their routines, from cleaning the ship to taking scientific samples, and to hunt for food. He even kept regular mealtimes and encouraged after-dinner conversation as a way to soothe everyone's nerves.

FOLLOWING HIS OWN PATH

Nothing in Ernest's upbringing prepared him for life on the high seas. He was the second child of ten born to a farm family in Kilkea, Ireland. When he was 6 years old, his dad made a big change: he went to Trinity College Dublin to become a doctor. When he qualified, he moved the family to Dublin and then South London to practice medicine. Ernest's dad wanted him to be a doctor, too, but Ernest wanted a different kind of life entirely. He had read about great adventures as a child, and he left in search of his own at 16 years old, joining the Merchant Navy and setting his own course for exploration.

But in October 1915—more than a year after they had left for Antarctica—the weakened hull of the *Endurance* began taking on water. Ernest ordered his crew to abandon ship, and they spent the night on the thick ice. The next day, he announced that they were going home. Exactly how they were going to accomplish that, he'd yet to figure out. But he was the leader of this group, and he knew he had to lead by example.

Ernest never let on how scared he was about the journey ahead. Instead, he put on a brave face and worked hard to keep everyone's spirits up. He also kept his crew focused on their new goal: to get home safely. When anyone would complain or argue, he assigned them to his own tent so they couldn't bring down the others. And finally, in April of 1916, the ice thawed enough to let them take their remaining lifeboats to the nearest piece of land they could find.

While the men enjoyed feeling their feet on dry land, Ernest started planning their next move. He sailed one of the lifeboats and five of the men 800 miles through rough, icy waters back to the port they'd left in 1914. A few went on to get help (and managed to grab a shower and some fresh clothes where they found it). But it took another few months to find a ship strong enough to get through the ice and back to the rest of the stranded crew. On August 30, 1916—a full 2 years after they first set sail—Ernest rescued his crew and took them home. Not a single life was lost.

TAKING RESPONSIBILITY

It's true that none of this might have happened if Ernest had planned better or listened to the warnings of the local sailors. But when you make a mistake, the only thing you can control is what you do next. Ernest took responsibility for his mistake, and he spent every day of that torturous 2-year-long ordeal making sure that none of his crew paid the price for it. He made a conscious decision to let go of dreams that didn't work out and to react well to whatever came his way. That decision and the effort that followed it saved 28 lives and made for far better inspiration to future explorers than a trek across the ice.

"DIFFICULTIES ARE JUST THINGS TO OVERCOME, AFTER ALL." —ERNEST SHACKLETON

R. BUCKMINSTER FULLER

ARCHITECT AND FUTURIST

BORN: 1895 · DIED: 1983

- Created the geodesic dome, an architectural wonder that was featured at the 1967 World Expo

- Received the Presidential Medal of Freedom for his contributions to society

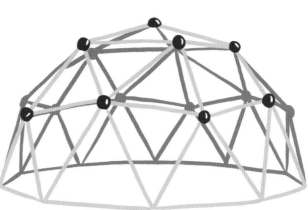

"I'M NOT A GENIUS. I'M JUST A TREMENDOUS BUNDLE OF EXPERIENCE." —R. BUCKMINSTER FULLER

If you've ever been on Spaceship Earth at Walt Disney World's Epcot, played on a climbing dome at the playground, or eaten in one of the heated igloos that popped up at restaurants all over during the COVID-19 pandemic, you've seen the work of famous inventor Richard Buckminster Fuller. Bucky, as he liked to be called, spent his whole life tinkering, designing, and innovating. But he came up with his greatest inventions (or *artifacts*, as he preferred to call them) after deciding to focus on helping people.

For someone who made a career out of geometric design, Bucky wasn't a fan of studying geometry at school. In fact, he wasn't a particularly engaged student at all. He was kicked out of Harvard University not once, but twice, for partying and a general lack of interest. But that was fine with Bucky—he preferred working with his hands anyway. He'd been making things out of found objects since he was a little boy, including using an umbrella to create a new system for rowing boats when he was 12 years old. After his first expulsion from Harvard, Bucky went to work at a local mill and got his machinist's certification. And after his second, he took what he'd learned to the U.S. Navy and invented a lifesaving winch for rescue boats that could quickly remove downed airplanes from the water.

In 1927, Bucky decided to try his hand at making the world a better place for everyone living in it. Bucky was a pioneer in sustainable design, realizing early on that resources were hard to come by in some areas of the world, and that they would only get more scarce as humanity used them up. He wanted not only to help those who needed innovation immediately but also to ensure that people were prepared for the future. To him, that meant doing more with less.

His first attempt was the Dymaxion house, a prefabricated round dwelling that would allow people to live efficiently and at a lower cost. (Dymaxion was short for Dynamic Maximum Tension, which basically means maximizing results while minimizing effort.) The house never caught on among average people, but the U.S. Army commissioned several for soldiers' use during World War II.

INSPIRING THE IMAGINEERS

There's a reason that Disney's own geodesic sphere (the building in Epcot that looks like a giant golf ball) houses a ride called "Spaceship Earth." Bucky inspired both. Disney imagineers knew they needed a spacious building for their flagship ride. When they turned to Bucky's geodesic design, they found the name for it, too, in his 1969 book titled *Operating Manual for Spaceship Earth*. In the book, Bucky refers to Earth as a magnificently designed spaceship and to humanity as its crew. (His point was that human beings need to work together to navigate life on Earth.) It's only fitting that the theme park Walt Disney designed as a haven for innovation would be home to one of Bucky's greatest designs.

The U.S. military remained one of Bucky's biggest customers, particularly when he created his most groundbreaking design: the geodesic dome. Geodesic domes (domes made up of small triangles) are lightweight, inexpensive, easy to assemble, and offer more interior space than traditional structures because they don't need any supporting beams. Plus, they distribute stress more evenly, making them stronger and more durable. A geodesic dome can survive a hurricane that would flatten many houses. Like the Dymaxion house, the domes didn't really catch on as private homes. But you can find them in other forms all over the world.

Bucky published his knowledge and experiences in nearly 30 books on design, materials, economics, philosophy, and—yes—even geometry. Although the geodesic dome is considered his greatest accomplishment, Bucky's true legacy is sustainable innovation. He got people thinking about how to use things like design and architecture to change the world for the better, and that's no small feat. As the world continues to change, many of us may find ourselves living in geodesic domes someday!

A GREATER PURPOSE

When Bucky's first business failed, he went into a deep depression. At 32 years old, he was unemployed, broke, ashamed, and desperate to provide for his wife and daughter. Bucky stood at the edge of Lake Michigan feeling hopeless; he decided he would throw himself in the water so that his wife could collect the money from his life insurance policy. But just before he did, he had an epiphany: he realized that if he died, all his knowledge, experience, and potential died with him. He thought, *What if I could change things for the better? Don't I owe it to the world to try?* From that moment on, Bucky decided to live his life with that greater purpose in mind. And he offered these words of wisdom for anyone feeling as hopeless and lost as he felt:

"Never forget that you are one of a kind. Never forget that if there weren't any need for you in all your uniqueness to be on this Earth, you wouldn't be here in the first place. And never forget, no matter how overwhelming life's challenges and problems seem to be, that one person can make a difference in the world. In fact, it is always because of one person that all the changes that matter in the world come about. So be that one person."

If you or someone you know is considering suicide, you're not alone. Call 1-800-273-8255 or go to www.suicidepreventionlifeline.org to talk to someone who can help.

WALT DISNEY

INNOVATOR AND ENTREPRENEUR

BORN: 1901 · DIED: 1966

- Created the Disney empire, which includes the film company and several theme parks around the world
- Produced the first-ever full-length animated movie (*Snow White and the Seven Dwarfs*)

"ALL OUR DREAMS CAN COME TRUE, IF WE HAVE THE COURAGE TO PURSUE THEM."

—WALT DISNEY

There's hardly a person alive who hasn't heard of Walt Disney. As the creator of Mickey Mouse, the Magic Kingdom, and the feature-length cartoon, he brought into being an empire that delights and inspires kids and adults all around the world. With all that success, you might think Walt had a sixth sense for it, that he knew exactly which projects and pursuits would pay off. But the truth was, Walt dreamed big and wasn't afraid to fail. And he failed a lot. From bankrupt businesses to films that bombed,

he took each setback in stride and got right back to work. Perseverance was the true secret to Walt Disney's success.

Walt fell in love with drawing when he was just a boy on his family's farm in Marceline, Missouri. But he was more than an artist; he was also already an entrepreneur at heart. He sold some of his early sketches to neighbors and traded others for things like haircuts. Selling his art was one of only a few of Walt's early ventures that succeeded. He also tried selling soda pop and candy to earn extra money, but he ended up eating and drinking most of his profits.

Walt's family moved several times, but Walt never stopped drawing and dreaming. While attending high school, he drew cartoons for his school newspaper and took classes at the Chicago Art Institute. Even as an ambulance driver in France at the end of World War I, he found time for his passion. He drew cartoons on the side of his truck, illustrated posters for the Red Cross, and even drew war-related cartoons for nationally published magazines like *Life*.

A HARD-WON WORK ETHIC

When Walt's dad got sick, he had to sell the farm and move his family to Kansas City to save money. Walt went from having an idyllic childhood surrounded by chickens and apple orchards to working his father's paper route at 4:30 a.m. And because his family needed the money from the route, Walt had to work other odd jobs in order to save any money for himself. By high school, he was taking art classes and working in a jelly factory in addition to doing his schoolwork. So, while Walt may have been born with his persevering spirit, he may also have developed it out of necessity.

By the time Walt was 18, he was employed full time as a cartoonist in Kansas City. A year later, he cofounded his own company with an illustrator he had met named Ub Iwerks. The company didn't last long, but the professional relationship did. Walt hired Ub as an animator at his next venture, Laugh-O-gram Films. That business failed fairly quickly, too.

Not to be deterred, Walt moved out to Hollywood, California, to start a new business with his brother Roy. They called it Disney Brothers Cartoon Studio, although it later became Walt Disney Studios. As soon as that business earned its first contract, Walt brought Ub on board, and together they created and refined the Mickey Mouse we know and love today.

Mickey wasn't just beloved; he was also a pioneer. "Steamboat Willie," the first cartoon to feature Mickey, was also the first production to synchronize sound and animation. Walt and Roy built on its success, incorporating newer technologies into their work and establishing Mickey as a national icon, ultimately creating the Disney brand.

In 1937, Walt took on his biggest project yet: the making of *Snow White and the Seven Dwarfs*. Back then, cartoons were meticulously hand-drawn, with each movement requiring a new sheet of paper with a new illustration. Those illustrations were then retraced in ink and filled with more than a thousand painted colors mixed just for the film. On top of that, the script, music, and sound effects had to be created. All in all, the film took 5 years and $1.5 million to make. Critics called the undertaking "Disney's Folly" and said that no one would want to watch a feature-length cartoon. But Walt's gamble paid off—the movie was a hit. And, of course, it wasn't the last.

As the Disney brand grew, Walt had another brilliant idea: to create a theme park based on his films. It wasn't all smooth sailing—opening day at Disneyland in 1955 was an absolute disaster, with bursting crowds and broken rides. But people felt its magic. Eventually, even presidents, kings, and queens would grace its manicured walkways. Of course, Walt had no way of knowing that when he began dreaming up his next big venture: Florida's Walt Disney World.

From drawing cartoons and voicing Mickey Mouse to inventing animated films and bringing their worlds to life, Walt had only one goal: to make people happy. He

STARTING OVER

With two failed businesses under his belt before starting Walt Disney Studios, Walt was no stranger to starting over. He had to do it again in 1928, when film distributor Charles Mintz hired the studio to develop a character called Oswald the Lucky Rabbit. Walt made Oswald a success, but Charles asserted his rights as owner of the trademark *and* tried to take over Walt Disney Studios. Walt instead abandoned Oswald and came up with his own character: Mickey Mouse. The rest was history! (The Walt Disney Company later gained the rights to Oswald, whom you can see in Disney's "Epic Mickey" video

didn't live to see Disney World built, but he would certainly have been proud of its evolution. Today, the Disney empire embodies all that Walt valued most: imagination, innovation, and joy.

ROBERTO BURLE MARX

LANDSCAPE ARCHITECT

BORN: 1909 · DIED: 1994

- Created thousands of visionary gardens and landscapes all over the world and discovered dozens of new plant species
- Advocated for the preservation of the Amazon rainforest

"CURIOSITY KEEPS ME ALIVE." —ROBERTO BURLE MARX

Life is a long and winding road, full of forks and stops, twists and bumps. You can choose to follow a map and go directly from A to B, or you can follow your curiosity and see where it leads you. Roberto Burle Marx chose the second option. By letting his curiosity inspire his journey, he created a life that was bigger, brighter, and more rewarding than he ever could have imagined.

Roberto fully intended to be a painter. At the age of 19, he traveled from his home of Rio de Janeiro, Brazil, to Berlin, Germany, to study art. But a few trips to the local botanical gardens changed everything. There, he saw the native plants of his home country and became enchanted all over again. Roberto had always loved plants, thanks to the encouragement of his mom and his governess, who taught him how to grow and appreciate them. He even grew and sold vegetables to earn enough money to buy and experiment with exotic plants when he was 15 years old. But seeing Brazil's plants in the structured setting of the botanical gardens stirred something in him.

When Roberto returned to Brazil, he found himself drawn to people who studied architecture and botany. It wasn't long before he designed his first landscape, a small private garden. Roberto quickly discovered he wasn't like other landscape architects. While they played it safe, using well-known plants and designs, he liked to be creative.

First and foremost, Roberto was still an artist; his medium just happened to be landscapes now. He wielded plants, paving stones, and water features like a painter wields his brushes, giving color and texture to his spaces and creating exceptional works of art. Once he was immersed in his lifelong passion, projects and praise followed quickly. He designed a roof garden for Brazil's Ministry of Education, the famous winding Copacabana promenade in Rio de Janeiro, the Cascade Garden at Longwood

Gardens in Pennsylvania, Biscayne Boulevard in Miami, Florida, and thousands of other gardens—each with its own personality.

Unlike a painter, however, Roberto needed an extensive knowledge of botany (the study of plants) to make his designs work. After all, these were living things he was incorporating between walkways and water features. They could be pretty particular about sunlight, soil, water intake, temperature, and proximity to other plants. Luckily, Roberto enjoyed cultivating plants as much as he enjoyed creating art.

With the rainforest nearby, Roberto went looking for inspiration often, even discovering new plant species along the way. He brought many plants home to study in his own private gardens, so that he could share the information he found with the world. There was no species too good or not good enough for Roberto. Experimentation and discovery were important parts of his artistic process, and they served his larger goal: conservation.

Roberto used his designs not only to create gorgeous spaces but also to bring awareness of the plants themselves. His designs included a mixture of native flora and plants from around the world so that people could enjoy them, learn about them, and want to protect them. With deforestation becoming a serious problem in the rainforests Roberto

A MAN OF MANY TALENTS

Roberto's artistic ability wasn't limited to landscape architecture. He engaged in music, painting, tapestry, sculpture, stage design, and even jewelry creation. A passion for art in all of its many forms is what drove Roberto to create the unique landscapes he became known for. Life (or, in Roberto's case, *living things*) imitated his art. His designs incorporated movement, in the form of colorful swirls and flowing water; structure, in towering stones and checkerboard lawns; and expression, in leafy plants and colorful blossoms.

regularly explored, he became an outspoken advocate for their preservation.

In 1969, Roberto said that the deforestation happening in the Amazon represented "an attack on humanity, an affront to the sources of life, and an assured means of destroying future generations." Even then, he understood what we know now: deforestation contributes to climate change, displaces Indigenous Peoples, and endangers the Amazon's 5,000 animal species and 40,000 plant species. Roberto's campaigns had a major impact on environmental laws and enforcement at the time and set a precedent for activists still fighting for the Amazon today.

By following his own curiosity, Roberto piqued the curiosity of others. He opened their eyes to the beauty of the world around them, as well as to its fragility. And by fighting against the destruction of the Amazon, he helped his fellow Brazilians see their rainforest as a national treasure, something to be protected and preserved. Today, Roberto's home is a UNESCO World Heritage Site (a place that's protected by the United Nations for its value to humanity) called Sítio Roberto Burle Marx, where more than 3,500 species of plants flourish and inspire future generations of artists and environmentalists.

LIVING ART

According to his protégée Raymond Jungles, Roberto "was always creating. That's what gave him joy." Raymond helped design the 2019 exhibition at the New York Botanical Gardens called "Brazilian Modern: The Living Art of Roberto Burle Marx," which honored Roberto's life through his history, his landscapes, and his artwork. Raymond was excited to share his friend's accomplishments, but he also believes Roberto's work is even more relevant today. As cities grow "more dense and less livable," Raymond says, people need ways to experience gardens and nature. Without access to spaces that demonstrate the wonders of the natural world, we're far less likely to fight for them.

JACQUES COUSTEAU

EXPLORER AND OCEANOGRAPHER

BORN: 1910 · DIED: 1997

- Known as the father of scuba diving, he helped develop the air regulator that allowed divers to dive freely
- Pioneered underwater filming, co-inventing the first true underwater camera

"THE SEA, ONCE IT CASTS ITS SPELL, HOLDS ONE IN ITS NET OF WONDER FOREVER."

—JACQUES COUSTEAU

What do you do when you can't find just the right thing for what you need? You create it. At least, that's how Jacques Cousteau saw things. He wanted to explore more of the oceans than anyone had before and to share their beauty with others on the surface. So, he created ways to do just that. And thanks to his inventions, we can all experience the wonders of underwater life, whether we want to dive in or stay on dry land.

Jacques loved exploring the underwater world, and he wanted more than anything to share its marvels with other people.

A CHILDHOOD HOBBY

Jacques had a bit of a rough time growing up. First, he had stomach issues that left him feeling weak. Then his father lost his job and his family experienced food insecurity. Even when things got better, Jacques didn't get excited about much. But he loved to make things. When Jacques was 11 years old, he made a working scale-model crane using plans from a magazine. And he didn't just build it, he also improved on the design. Jacques held onto that ingenuity and love of engineering throughout his life, contributing to a number of inventions that improved diving for explorers and filmmakers like himself.

Before 1943, divers had to be tethered to boats and receive oxygen from tanks onboard. Jacques and French engineer Émile Gagnan experimented until they found a solution: the Aqua-Lung and its breathing regulator. Divers could carry tanks on their backs and receive air as needed and at the right pressure, freeing them from the hoses and heavy helmets to explore farther. That made scuba diving more accessible to more people, including the millions who use the same setup today.

LOVE AT FIRST SIGHT

Jacques was always an explorer at heart, but he never imagined exploring the oceans. In fact, he joined the French Navy to become a naval aviator. But a bad car crash and two broken arms dashed his hopes when he was 26 years old. A friend suggested swimming as a way for Jacques to heal and strengthen his arms. One day, that friend offered Jacques use of his snorkel and mask, and Jacques discovered an entire world beneath the water's surface. Jacques said that's when he fell in love with the ocean.

Once Jacques could explore more of the oceans, he wanted to document more of them. He had loved filmmaking since he got his first camera (and one of the *first-ever* personal video cameras) when he was 13. But now he needed a camera and lighting that would work underwater at the greatest depths. He collaborated with a professor named Harold Edgerton at the Massachusetts Institute of Technology to create lights that could penetrate deep, dark waters (where no sunlight can reach from the surface). Then, in 1961, he helped create the first true underwater camera, which he named Calypso, after his ship.

Jacques didn't just take pictures underwater. He made stunning colorized films that allowed audiences to see the oceans like never before. The films show giant pods of dolphins jumping alongside boats, lobsters hiding in deep crevices, and colorful tropical fish flitting through the water. They also showed the dangers of scuba diving and the sometimes-frightening power of the oceans.

Jacques's creations allowed people to uncover the mysteries of the ocean, which not only aided scientific research but also helped people understand and care about marine life. As Jacques put it, "People protect what they love." And the oceans, he realized, needed protection. In 1959, he discovered that the French government was considering dumping nuclear waste in the ocean. He immediately set to work to make sure everyone knew of the proposal. In the face of overwhelming opposition, the government conceded. In the 1970s, Jacques started to sound a wider alarm. For decades, he'd watched reefs dying and species of fish disappearing.

Jacques understood what few others did: that the damage we do today will affect the generations to come. In 1992, he gave a passionate speech at a UN conference, saying, "Let us cease thinking only of ourselves and reasoning only in the short term. . . . This is our responsibility, as we hold in our hands the future of tomorrow's exacting generations." And in 1997, the year Jacques died, the UN made a declaration to act accordingly.

Jacques wasn't a scientist. He wasn't even a conservationist at first. He was just a man who loved the ocean and had a knack for making things. Jacques shared his discoveries, inventions, and passion with the world in the hopes that we would fall in love just like he did, and then fight just like he did. Because, as Jacques has shown us, the oceans and all of their incredible inhabitants are worth fighting for.

DO BETTER

Maya Angelou once said, "Do the best you can until you know better. Then when you know better, do better." Jacques certainly lived by that philosophy. In his early years of exploring the oceans, he put discovery above conservation and caring for living creatures. In fact, he and his team could be rather cruel to the creatures they came across. But the more Jacques studied marine creatures and their environment, the more he realized that human beings were having a devastating impact on them. By the end of his life, he was a vocal and determined champion for the oceans and the creatures that call them home.

JONAS SALK

MEDICAL RESEARCHER

BORN: 1914 · DIED: 1995

- Developed the first safe polio vaccine
- Declined to patent the vaccine so that as many people as possible could get it

"HOPE LIES IN DREAMS, IN IMAGINATION, AND IN THE COURAGE OF THOSE WHO DARE TO MAKE DREAMS INTO REALITY." –JONAS SALK

There's no magic formula for becoming a trailblazer, but being surrounded by loving, supportive people can certainly help. Just look at Louis Braille (page 19) or Colin Kaepernick (page 111). And don't worry if you face a few naysayers. They can help, too, by pushing you to find your own voice, your own strength, and your own path. Jonas Salk did. By choosing to stand his ground in the face of doubt and disapproval, he changed the course of history and saved countless lives in the process.

The person who tore Jonas down was the same person who really wanted to lift him up: his mom. Just like Jonas, Dora Salk had been a smart and capable kid, but she didn't have opportunities to learn and grow. As the child of Jewish immigrants just arrived in the United States, she went to work in a garment factory to help support her family.

When she became a mother, she wanted better futures for her children. She knew that Jonas had greatness in him. As he grew, he was quiet, thoughtful, and well-behaved (unlike his younger brothers). He was also a whiz at school, skipping multiple grades. Mother and son would sit and have long conversations about the world. But Dora could be overbearing at times—she had strong opinions and high expectations. And Jonas bore the brunt of her criticism.

From the time Jonas was a little boy, he had a strong desire to make a difference in the world. He wanted to relieve some of the suffering that seemed to be all around him. (He lived through both World War I and the Great Depression.) After thinking about ways he could make an impact, Jonas decided to change his field of study from literature to law. But he didn't dare mention the switch to his mom.

A PRODUCTIVE ESCAPE

Polio was at its worst during the warm summer months, so pools and playgrounds closed, and kids were often kept safely at home. Jonas found the perfect escape: reading. He was never without a book. That love of learning, combined with his natural cleverness, helped him skip several grades, and he found himself starting college before his 16th birthday. He was the first person in his family to go to college.

Jonas kept his head down and focused completely on his schoolwork to keep his grades up. And when he finally worked up the courage to tell his mother what he was working toward, she took the wind right out of his sails by pointing out that he couldn't even win an argument against *her*. Dejected, he switched his course of study again, this time to medicine.

After years with his nose in great novels, Jonas was pleasantly surprised by how much he enjoyed studying science. But his mom shot him down again, telling him he didn't have the stomach for medicine. This time, however, he decided to prove her wrong.

In medicine, Jonas finally found a way to alleviate some of the world's suffering. A terrifying virus called polio had plagued the summers since Jonas was just 2 years old. It affected children more than anyone, killing many and often paralyzing those who survived. Some had too little muscle function to breathe on their own and had to live in iron lungs—giant machines that stimulate breathing. There was no cure.

After some success with flu vaccines, Jonas decided to try his hand at one for polio. Up until this point, vaccines were made up of a bit of live virus that would essentially teach your immune system how to recognize the virus and kill it. But because it was

"THE REWARD FOR WORK WELL DONE IS THE OPPORTUNITY TO DO MORE." –JONAS SALK

live, there was still some risk of people becoming infected. Jonas had a different idea: what if vaccines used a bit of virus that's already been killed? Would your body react the same way? The answer was a resounding yes.

Jonas was so confident about his polio vaccine that he tested it on himself, his wife, and their children. Every one of them developed antibodies to the virus (blood proteins that fight off the virus) without any trace of the virus itself. In 1954, Jonas expanded testing to include one million children between the ages of 6 and 9, who were called the Polio Pioneers. Desperate for an end to polio, people across the country were happy to volunteer.

On April 12, 1955, banner headlines exclaimed that a safe, effective vaccine was poised to make polio a thing of the past. And it did. In the United States today, polio is a distant memory for

A SENSE OF PURPOSE

The same sense of purpose that led Jonas to develop the vaccine also led him to forgo profits. He wanted to make sure everyone who needed the vaccine could get it. By refusing to patent his creation, he allowed anyone to make it, and he freely gave them the information to do it. To him, ending polio was worth more than any amount of money he could earn from it.

most adults and completely unknown to most kids. And it's all thanks to Jonas's actively looking for ways to help and nurturing a seed that no one else could imagine blossoming.

NELSON MANDELA

PRESIDENT OF SOUTH AFRICA

BORN: 1918 · DIED: 2013

- South Africa's first democratically elected president and winner of a Nobel Peace Prize
- Helped bring an end to apartheid, South Africa's system of racial segregation

> "I LEARNED THAT COURAGE WAS NOT THE ABSENCE OF FEAR, BUT THE TRIUMPH OVER IT. THE BRAVE MAN IS NOT HE WHO DOES NOT FEEL AFRAID, BUT HE WHO CONQUERS THAT FEAR." —NELSON MANDELA

Change is not always a quick or an easy process. For Nelson Mandela, the South African icon who helped bring an end to the racist government policy of apartheid, it was a process that took roughly 40 years. But with patience and perseverance, he helped change the course of history for his entire country.

When Nelson was born, South Africa was harshly segregated: the white minority (who had colonized the area centuries earlier) had control over the Black majority. But as a child, Nelson didn't know anything about that. He only knew the comforts of his village, which had existed much the same way for centuries as part of the

Xhosa nation. Nelson's dad was a chief of the Thembu people, which meant that Nelson was a member of the tribe's royal family.

Nelson was a bright and curious kid who loved to explore the land around his village. He fished and foraged, tended to the sheep and cows, swam in the cool streams, and got into plenty of trouble with friends. But all that changed when his dad died. His mom told him to pack his things and walked him up to the Great Place, home to Jongintaba Dalindyebo, the ruler of the Thembu people. As a friend of Nelson's dad, Jongintaba had offered to be Nelson's guardian.

ABOUT APARTHEID

The word "apartheid" means "apartness" in Afrikaans, a language used in South Africa that evolved from the language used by Dutch settlers. Apartheid became the law of the land in 1948. Black South Africans were not allowed to mix with or marry white South Africans and were also sent to live apart from each other so that they couldn't rise up together. Black South Africans who worked in white areas were required to show documents authorizing them to be in the white areas. Black people had no say in their own government, which stole land from its Black citizens. From 1961 to 1994, more than 3.5 million Black people were expelled from their homes. When Black citizens stood up to the government, they were often jailed or killed.

long before Nelson found his voice as an activist, and he was expelled from school for protesting the student government. His choice was to return home to an arranged marriage or to start fresh somewhere else. Nelson fled to Soweto, where he became a part-time law student and, at the same time, started the country's first Black law firm. He also joined the African National Congress, which fought for the rights of Black South Africans.

Following the path of Mohandas Gandhi (page 31), Nelson first tried to fight apartheid through nonviolent protests, boycotts, and civil disobedience. His activism started to make headlines internationally, but he and 8,000 others were jailed. When he got out of jail, he continued to fight and was arrested again. Nelson's trial went on for 5 years. Although Nelson was found not guilty, he went into hiding for 17 months, hoping to plan his next moves without government interference.

Spurred on by the deadly shootings of Black protestors by police, Nelson and other activists concluded that peaceful protests might not be the best way forward. Nelson had just been to see Nobel Peace Prize winner Chief Albert Luthuli

Living at the Great Place helped Nelson learn about the world and grow into a leader like his dad. It also helped him get a spot at the only Black university in South Africa. But it wasn't to talk about armed rebellion when he was arrested for leaving the country without his documentation. When police discovered his plans, he was charged with sabotage.

Nelson and his fellow activists knew they faced a death sentence, so they decided to turn their trials into a show for the whole world to see. Nelson himself gave a passionate 4-hour speech during his testimony, saying, "The lack of human dignity experienced by Africans is the direct result of the policy of white supremacy." The prisoners made sure that the world knew what they were fighting for: a free society for *all* people in South Africa. Nelson was sentenced to life in prison, but he'd gotten the world's attention.

For 27 years, in his prison cell, Nelson remained a powerful figure in the anti-apartheid movement. His supporters never stopped calling for his release. And by the mid-1970s, the rest of the world had started calling for an end to South Africa's racist policies. Between the resistance from South African citizens and the pressure from countries like the United Kingdom and the United States, South Africa's new president F.W. de Klerk could see the writing on the wall. He freed Nelson from prison and, together, they brought an end to apartheid. Nelson Mandela, now known as the father of South Africa, became its first democratically elected president just 3 years later.

A MAN OF MANY NAMES

Nelson's father actually named him Rolihlahla at birth (a name that translates as "troublemaker" in his native Xhosa), but his father never got to see how fitting the name truly was. Rolihlahla received the name Nelson on his first day at the English school, and the name Dalibhunga during his tribal initiation a few years later. While he was on the run, the South African media dubbed him "The Black Pimpernel." Others called him by his clan's name, Mandiba, out of respect. But the world knew him as Nelson Mandela, the name given to him by the oppressive system he spent his life fighting.

ALAN SHEPARD

ASTRONAUT

BORN: 1923 · DIED: 1998

- The first American in space and the fifth person in history to walk on the moon
- Helped found the Mercury Seven Foundation, now called the Astronaut Scholarship Foundation

"WHEN I FIRST LOOKED BACK AT THE EARTH, STANDING ON THE MOON, I CRIED."

—ALAN SHEPARD

Before the Wright brothers (page 27) invented the airplane in 1903, no one knew that human flight was possible. Yet, by 1959, people were engaged in space programs, which aimed to launch human beings beyond Earth's own atmosphere. This was completely new territory. Space program scientists had theories and math, but they didn't have experience. It took a special kind of person to sign up for that gig. The person had to have experience, certainly. But they also needed to have a love of flying and lots of faith, both in science and in their own abilities.

Alan Shepard was that kind of person. Not only was he an excellent pilot, having logged 8,000 hours in flight as a test pilot for the Navy, but also he was highly competitive and self-assured. His high IQ and his infatuation with flight as a child seemed to indicate that Alan was destined for NASA (which didn't exist until 1958). Alan founded a model airplane club at his high school, received a flight in a DC-3 as a Christmas gift when he was 15, and rode his bicycle to the local airfield to do odd jobs in exchange for informal flight lessons.

A LITTLE COMPETITION

Alan was the first American in space, but he wasn't the first person in space. That accomplishment belongs to Russian cosmonaut Yuri Gagarin, who went to space a whopping 23 days before Alan. But because Yuri's flight was managed by space control on the ground, Alan was the first person to pilot a spacecraft himself. The excitement of the space race inspired every astronaut to go farther and to discover more about space than anyone had before.

After attending the Naval Academy, fighting in World War II, and showing incredible skill as a test pilot, Alan was chosen (out of more than 100 recruits) by NASA for its first-ever team of astronauts. Alan joined the Mercury 7, which included John Glenn, Virgil "Gus" Grissom, Donald "Deke" Slayton, Malcolm "Scott" Carpenter, Walter "Wally" Schirra, and Gordon Cooper. But only Alan was selected to pilot the first flight into space. At the time, NASA administrators said it was because they wanted to put their best foot forward.

In Alan's first foray into space aboard the *Freedom 7*,

he reached an altitude of 116 miles during his 15-minute suborbital flight. (The average plane flies at an altitude of less than 7 miles today.) Then he plummeted back to Earth, landing in the Atlantic Ocean near the Bahamas.

Alan went on to help other astronauts make space flights before NASA moved on to the next phase in their plan to put a man on the moon. That phase, called Gemini, aimed to ready the astronauts to dock spacecraft in orbit and to perform spacewalks on the moon. Alan himself was all set to participate in Gemini 3, the first manned Gemini mission, when he woke up to a terrible surprise: he was suffering from a dizzying disorder called Ménière's disease, causing him to feel nauseated and unsteady on his feet. He was grounded. Not one to sit around, Alan took up the post of chief of the Astronaut Office for NASA, helping to plan the missions and oversee the training of the astronauts involved.

Six years later, in 1969, Alan underwent a brand-new operation that completely relieved his dizziness and other symptoms. Because of the timing of Alan's surgery, he didn't have enough training to fly on the next mission: the ill-fated *Apollo 13*. That mission never made it to the moon, being forced to return after an oxygen-tank explosion. But *Apollo 14* did make it to the moon, and Alan was on it.

Apollo 14 left Cape Canaveral on January 31, 1971, and astronauts landed on the lunar surface on February 7. Alan and another astronaut, Ed Mitchell, spent more than 33 hours on the moon—the longest amount of time yet—and more than 9 hours outside of their spacecraft. After their mission was complete, Alan unfolded a telescoping golf club and hit two golf balls across the surface of the moon. One landed in a crater, but the other traveled an impressive 218 yards. (The longest golf shot here on Earth, where gravity keeps the ball moving forward, measured 475 yards.) Back in Florida, Alan spent the rest of his NASA career training future moonwalkers.

Despite being a trailblazer, Alan never liked the spotlight. He was a very private person, and he refused to cash in on his career. (He also didn't need to, having made quite a bit of money in banking and real estate after leaving NASA.) He simply believed in the work. As he put it once, "Whether you are an astronomer or a life scientist, geophysicist, or a pilot, you've got to be

A SECOND CHANCE

It's a good thing that Alan got to go to space more than once. On his first spaceflight, he was strapped so tightly in his seat that he didn't get to experience weightlessness. And the portholes were positioned so that he couldn't even catch a glimpse of the stars. He couldn't even see the blue of Earth's oceans because a filter on the periscope window made everything look black and white.

there because you believe you are good in your field, and you can contribute, not because you are going to get a lot of fame or whatever when you get back." Alan's natural intelligence and competitive drive certainly helped him move effortlessly from one incredible task to the next. But it was his faith in himself and his abilities that drove him.

DAVID ATTENBOROUGH

EXPLORER AND NATURALIST

BORN: 1926

- Inventor of the nature documentary
- One of the first people to call attention to humanity's impact on the natural world

"AN UNDERSTANDING OF THE NATURAL WORLD IS A SOURCE OF NOT ONLY GREAT CURIOSITY BUT GREAT FULFILLMENT." —DAVID ATTENBOROUGH

Can you imagine going fossil hunting for weeks at a time all by yourself? Or going fossil hunting at all? But that was how 13-year-old David Attenborough spent most of his time. He'd take off on his bike to spend weeks scouring the Lake District in northwest England for creatures that lived 150 million years ago just as easily as he'd bike over to nearby fields to watch the birds. (Times were different back then, and his parents were on board with his long bike trips.) David was just completely fascinated by nature.

SNEAKY BUSINESS

When David was 11 years old, he made a tidy sum of money selling newts to the zoology department of the local university. Scientists there needed a large number of them for their research, and David knew just where to find them. What David didn't tell the scientists was that he pulled the newts from a pond right next to the university. Keeping a watchful eye on nature has its rewards!

David's collection of fossils caught the eye of future archeologist Jacquetta Hawkes, who was happy to see someone taking an interest in the subject. She encouraged David by sending him a package full of goodies to add to his homemade museum, including a dried seahorse, a piece of Roman pottery, and an ancient coin. Her support made all the difference—that's when David decided he'd become a naturalist (someone who studies natural history), and he did.

Today, you might know David Attenborough as the kind, white-haired gentleman whose soothing voice washes over sweeping documentary scenes of animals in stunning natural habitats. In fact, David was the first to create such a televised marvel. He filmed *Life on Earth*, the first-ever natural history documentary, in 1979. And an incredible 500 million people watched it, hungry for more. With more than 100 documentaries to his name, David has been meeting that demand ever since and continues to work tirelessly to save our planet in the process.

David started his career in television by joining the BBC (the British Broadcasting Corporation) as an intern in 1954, having

watched only one TV show in his life. But, as a born adventurer, he wasn't about to sit in the studio all day. He asked his bosses if he could create a nature program—one that would get him outside at least some of the time. That program was a series called "Zoo Quest," which gave viewers a look at wild animals like Komodo dragons and chimpanzees. The show was a hit, proving to reluctant TV executives that wildlife programs were well worth making.

That was the spark that led David to make a career of creating incredible nature documentaries and inspiring generations of people to discover the wonders around them. After 20 years climbing the corporate ladder at the BBC, David went back to doing what he loved: exploring the natural world. In front of the camera once again, he took viewers all over the world. He showed them not only plants and animals but also some of the most remote tribes of people on the planet. His work helped viewers see the world from a new perspective.

In the decades that have followed, David has shown viewers many more parts of the world—on land, in the air, and underwater—than they might ever have seen without his nature documentaries. In

fact, over the length of his career, David has caught several species on camera for the first time in history. And learning about the creatures that have inhabited Earth, whether they're fossilized or newly discovered, is essential for gaining a better understanding of the planet. We can uncover more of our history, protect our ecosystems, and even develop better medications as a result.

While sharing his love of the natural world with millions of viewers, David has also shared a stark warning: humans are doing irreparable harm to nature. But he hasn't lost hope. In a 2021 speech at a worldwide climate summit, David said, "In my lifetime, I've witnessed a terrible decline. In yours, you could and should witness a wonderful recovery." He urged people all over the world to fight for the health of the planet with the reminder that we are "the greatest problem solvers to have ever existed on the Earth."

David didn't set out to save the world. He simply enjoyed observing its inhabitants— watching gorillas roll around in lush mountain vegetation, polar bears slide through the snow, and birds of paradise fluff their colorful feathers. By continuing to explore and to push further into the

wilderness, he came to realize that much of what he saw and loved was in danger of disappearing. David hopes that, by showing people what wonders exist in the natural world, he'll inspire us to preserve it. And thanks to him, there's plenty of inspiring video to be seen.

WHAT'S IN A NAME?

In his lifetime, David has traveled nearly 2 million miles and visited 94 countries. Unsurprisingly, David has discovered quite a few species of plants and animals during his trips, and he has had the honor of naming more than a few. And, as an inspiration to scientists and naturalists, he's even had a few named after *him*, including a beetle, an entire genus of flowering plant, and a long-necked, water-dwelling dinosaur called the Attenborosaurus. The United Kingdom also named a polar research ship after him: the RSS *Sir David Attenborough*.

FRED ROGERS

TELEVISION PIONEER

BORN: 1928 · DIED: 2003

- Created *Mister Rogers' Neighborhood*, a pioneering television program for children
- Helped save public television by testifying before a Senate subcommittee

"LISTENING IS WHERE LOVE BEGINS: LISTENING TO OURSELVES AND THEN TO OUR NEIGHBORS." –FRED ROGERS

Some people seem like they're born knowing exactly what they want to do with their life and how to get there. Others take their time figuring out which path to take. They try new things, pursue different interests, see which possible future feels best. But what if you can't choose? With a little luck and a lot of creativity, you might just find a way to do it all.

Take Fred Rogers, for example. He found a way to combine music, writing, art, faith, kindness, conservation, and education into a career that accomplished his greatest goal in life: to help children thrive. The result was *Mister Rogers' Neighborhood*, an iconic

and beloved show of Fred's own creation that spent an astonishing 33 years on air.

Fred wrote and hosted all 895 episodes of the show, wrote more than 200 songs for it, and created 14 puppets to help kids learn and grow through play, music, stories, and conversation. He purposely put his many talents front and center. By embracing his interests, he encouraged his viewers to embrace theirs. As Fred put it, "As human beings, our job in life is to help people realize how rare and valuable each one of us really is, that each of us has something that no one else has—or ever will have—something inside that is unique to all time."

"REAL STRENGTH HAS TO DO WITH HELPING OTHERS."

—FRED ROGERS

WORDS OF WISDOM

The real Mr. McFeely also inspired the lines Fred used to close out his show at the end of every episode. Fred's grandfather once said to him, "You know, you made this day a really special day. Just by being yourself. There's only one person in the world like you. And I happen to like you just the way you are." For three decades, Fred looked into the camera and offered the same compliment to millions of children, who took it to heart, just like he had.

struggling and took the boy under his wing, inspiring not only his grandson's self-esteem but also his entire career. Many of the characters and lessons on *Mister Rogers' Neighborhood* came from those lonely times, including Mr. McFeely: the delivery man named for Fred's grandfather.

Thanks in large part to his grandfather, Fred had found his confidence by high school. He'd become a good student, an accomplished musician, and even student council president in his senior year. When he went off to college, his plan was to study music before becoming a minister. But coming home on break during college and finding a TV in his family's living room changed everything. As soon as Fred saw the new technology, he understood its potential.

Fred used his music degree and his many talents to break into the broadcasting industry and to create innovative shows for kids on public television. First, he developed a program called *The Children's Corner*. Then, in 1963, he moved to Canada and started working in front of the camera on a similar program called *Misterogers*. Those shows laid the groundwork for his return to Pittsburgh and the creation of *Mister Rogers' Neighborhood* in 1966.

That's a lesson that Fred himself had to learn as a child. Growing up, Fred was shy, sensitive, and overweight, and due to terrible seasonal allergies, he was often stuck inside while other kids were playing outside. He felt alone a lot of the time. Thankfully, Fred's grandfather noticed him

With a flair all his own, Fred taught viewers (and not just kids) how to feel their feelings, be themselves, discover the world, and treat each other with kindness—and he led by example. In one landmark episode, Fred invited Officer Clemmons to join him in soaking his feet in a wading pool. That might not sound very exciting, but the episode aired in 1969 amid a nationwide battle over segregated swimming pools, and Officer Clemmons was Black. Fred's simple act of sharing his time and space with Officer Clemmons was more than just a lesson in kindness; it was also a trailblazing public statement against racism.

That wasn't the first or the last time Fred made headlines. That same year, he appeared before the U.S. Senate Subcommittee on Communication to argue against drastic budget cuts to public television. Fred didn't use big words or complicated arguments to sway the chairman of the subcommittee. He simply told the chairman what his show was about. But he gave the

chairman goosebumps all the same and won his argument.

Fred once said that learning he could use all of his talents to help children made him feel whole. But it made them feel whole, too. When he retired in 2001, he left behind a legacy of learning, kindness, respect, and self-worth that inspired not only generations of viewers but also the future of children's entertainment and education.

LEARNING TO TEACH

Fred never stopped educating himself, even after he became the star, writer, and producer of his own show. First, he became an ordained minister with a specialization in children and families. Then he began studying child development at the University of Pittsburgh and forged relationships with child psychologists who would help him develop the content for his show. Fred felt it was his responsibility to keep learning in order to offer his viewers the best advice possible.

THEOLOGY 101

SPEECH
WINNER

MARTIN LUTHER KING JR.

CIVIL RIGHTS LEADER

BORN: 1929 · DIED: 1968

- Received the Nobel Peace Prize at the age of 35 and used the money to further the fight for civil rights
- Fought for racial equality through nonviolent demonstrations

"DARKNESS CANNOT DRIVE OUT DARKNESS; ONLY LIGHT CAN DO THAT. HATE CANNOT DRIVE OUT HATE; ONLY LOVE CAN DO THAT." –MARTIN LUTHER KING JR.

Martin Luther King Jr. was many things—a minister, a community leader, a writer, and a civil rights icon. But long before that, he was just a boy who believed things could be different. He spent his life looking for ways to make life better for Black people across the country. And because he *believed* he could change the world, he did.

Martin grew up in Atlanta, Georgia, at a time when segregation was the law of the land. That meant that, as long as the facilities were equal, people could be separated from each other by the color of their skin. Bathrooms, drinking fountains, businesses, and schools were segregated into "Black" and "white." Things were rarely equal, though, and Black people were always expected to accommodate whites.

For example, on public buses, the front half of each bus was reserved for whites, while the back half was designated for Blacks. If no seats were available when a white passenger got on, Black passengers were expected to clear a row and spend the ride standing so that the white passenger could sit. Martin's dad understandably hated this practice, and he encouraged his son to avoid taking the bus whenever possible.

By the age of 15, Martin had had enough of segregated buses, too. On a long trip home from winning a public speaking competition, he was told to make room for white passengers. He refused. Knowing that Martin could have been hurt or even jailed for resisting, his teacher finally persuaded him to move. But Martin said it was the angriest he'd ever been in his life.

That experience fueled his desire to put an end to segregated buses, and he knew that getting the right education was the first crucial step. After receiving a degree in sociology from Morehouse College, he threw himself into religious studies at Crozer Theological Seminary (to the delight of his father, who'd always hoped Martin would follow in his footsteps as a preacher). He read everything he could get his hands on and even went on to get his doctorate in systematic theology at Boston University.

AN EARLY EDUCATION

When Martin was 5 years old, his white friends went off to their white schools and weren't allowed to play with him anymore. Martin couldn't understand it. That's when his mother taught him about slavery and segregation. But she also taught him to hold his head high and to know that, no matter the law, he was as good as any white person. Despite living in the deeply segregated South and facing discrimination often, both of Martin's parents believed wholeheartedly in racial equality. That belief helped Martin become a strong, committed leader who made history.

In Boston, Martin met and married his wife, Coretta Scott. Although they found that Black citizens had more freedom and respect in the North, the pair felt strongly that they were needed in the South. History proved them right just a year later, when a woman named Rosa Parks refused to give up her seat on a segregated bus. Martin leapt into action as a leader of the National Association for the Advancement of Colored People (NAACP) and helped organize the Montgomery Bus Boycott, which brought an end to the segregated bus system. To continue the fight for racial equality, he helped found the Southern Christian Leadership Conference (SCLC) in 1957 and, soon after, became its president.

Despite his anger, Martin advocated for a new way to create change—one that relied on peaceful demonstrations and nonviolent civil disobedience. This was a combination of the tenets of Christianity and the philosophies of another historic leader: Mohandas Gandhi (page 31). Martin and Coretta even traveled to India in 1959 to learn more about Gandhi's teachings and to bring those lessons home to strengthen the civil rights movement.

From 1957 until his death in 1968, Martin traveled more than 6 million miles to learn, to lead protests, and to organize voter registration. He spoke publicly 2,500 times and wrote five books and many more articles. In other words, he did whatever it took to fight for justice and peace. His activism directly contributed to the creation of the Civil Rights Act of 1964 and the Voting Rights Act of 1965,

PRACTICE MAKES POWERFUL

Martin Luther King Jr. was known for being an incredible and inspiring public speaker. But he wasn't just born with that gift—he worked hard to develop it. At the seminary where he studied to become a preacher, he would spend hours practicing his sermons in the mirror. That dedication and hard work helped him not only graduate at the top of his mostly white class but also become one of the most respected leaders in history.

which formally ended segregation, banned workplace discrimination, and helped ensure access to voting for Black citizens.

Although he was an advocate for peace, Martin's work made him the target of violence and threats. In 1968, Martin was shot and killed while standing on the balcony of his Memphis motel room. His death devastated those who saw Martin as a beacon of hope for a better future. But his message of love and equality has lived on and has echoed throughout history. Today, it gives the organizers and activists who have come after him not just a template for their work but also the motivation to keep doing it, because they know it can change the world.

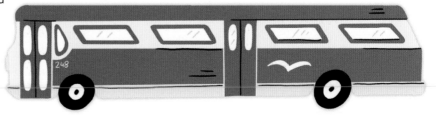

HARVEY MILK

LGBTQ+ ACTIVIST

BORN: 1930 · DIED: 1978

- One of the first openly gay politicians to be elected to government office in the United States
- Gave the LGBTQ+ community hope that they could be themselves and change the world

"ALL YOUNG PEOPLE, REGARDLESS OF SEXUAL ORIENTATION OR IDENTITY, DESERVE A SAFE AND SUPPORTIVE ENVIRONMENT IN WHICH TO ACHIEVE THEIR FULL POTENTIAL."

—HARVEY MILK

When you feel like you're different from other people, it can be tempting to try to blend in. Invisibility offers protection and safety. Maybe you hug the wall at the school dance, or you sit at the back of the class so you won't be called on. Maybe you keep your opinion to yourself when you really want to speak up. But what if you knew there were other people just like you who were hiding, too? By being yourself, you can encourage others to be themselves. And together, you can face anything.

That's how Harvey Milk felt about coming out as gay—that it gave others in the LGBTQ+ community the chance to be themselves, too. But that was often easier said than done. Harvey grew up at a time, not all that long ago, when being gay almost guaranteed a life of hardship. Either you hid who you were or you risked being discriminated against in almost every aspect of your life. You could lose your job, be ejected from the military, or even be thrown in jail for admitting to being gay. The LGBTQ+ community had no legal rights. And that's exactly what Harvey set out to change.

They say the third time's the charm. It took *four* elections for Harvey to finally win a seat on the San Francisco Board of Supervisors. But he knew that he would win eventually if he just kept trying, and that winning was too important to the LGTBQ+ community for him to give up. It didn't hurt that Harvey grew up with the kind of family that made him believe he could succeed at anything he put his mind to.

HIDING IN PLAIN SIGHT

Harvey's family had no idea he was gay, but he knew he was before he entered high school. In high school, he was popular, charismatic, athletic, and very much in the closet. He dated girls and kept his friends at arm's length. He also worked very hard to graduate early so that he could start college and, possibly, have a chance to be himself. But in the 1940s and '50s, there was nowhere Harvey would be safe coming out of the closet. It took decades for him to find the strength to come out and to be a vocal advocate for the LGBTQ+ community.

Harvey was born into a well-respected, middle-class Jewish family in Woodmere, New York. His parents had served in the Navy. His grandfather owned a local department store and helped found a Jewish synagogue. The entire family was known for giving back to their community. Harvey's mom, Minerva, attributed that to the Jewish principle of *tikkun olam*, which means "repair the world" in Hebrew, and which refers to the practice of working to right the world's wrongs, usually through volunteer work and activism. Harvey inherited his mother's commitment to making the world a better, more just place.

Harvey first chose to serve the world by joining the Navy, like his parents. But he was forced to resign when superiors learned he was gay, and he was given an "other than honorable" discharge. (Many years later, the Navy offered to change that to an honorable discharge, but Harvey's nephew declined on his behalf. He felt it was important that the history stand so people could learn from it.) Harvey held a few different jobs, from teacher to

investment banker to camera-shop owner, before running for office from the Castro neighborhood of San Francisco.

Harvey made it clear that he wanted to improve life for everyone. His platform included opening daycare centers for working families, creating more low-cost housing, attracting new business to the area, and advocating for safer neighborhoods. Harvey was elected to office in 1977. Sadly, he had less than a year in office before he was assassinated alongside Mayor George Moscone by a fellow city supervisor who was both anti-gay and angry at the mayor. Harvey had known that being an openly gay official meant putting his life on the line, but he believed his work was worth the risk.

We have a long way to go toward offering the LGBTQ+ community equal rights and protections under the law and accepting

A LASTING IMPRESSION

Harvey grew up during World War II, when Nazis were actively trying to exterminate Jewish and gay people like him. When he was a teen, his parents told him the story of the Warsaw Uprising. The Nazis were holding thousands of Jewish people in a ghetto in Warsaw, Poland, only to send them to their deaths. One day, the prisoners rebelled. They were weak from being tortured and had few weapons, but they fought bravely against their captors and created months of chaos that weakened the Nazis and made the rest of the world pay attention. The moral of the story was that, although the captives knew they would most likely die either way, they chose to die fighting. They chose to sacrifice themselves to save others. And that's a lesson that Harvey carried with him for the rest of his life.

its members the way Harvey had wanted. But Harvey did what he set out to do: he gave the LGBTQ+ community hope. Thanks in part to his hard work and dedication, there are roughly 1,000 openly LGBTQ+ elected officials in the United States today.

"HOPE WILL NEVER BE SILENT." –HARVEY MILK

BILL GATES

INNOVATOR AND PHILANTHROPIST

BORN: 1955

- Cofounded Microsoft, the world's largest personal software company
- Created the Bill & Melinda Gates Foundation to fight poverty, disease, and inequity around the world

"SURROUND YOURSELF WITH PEOPLE WHO CHALLENGE YOU, TEACH YOU, AND PUSH YOU TO BE YOUR BEST SELF."

—BILL GATES

Have you ever played Xbox? Used Microsoft Windows? Written something in a Word document? Then you have Bill Gates to thank. Today, he's an icon of innovation and one of the richest men alive. But he started out just like you—a smart kid with a great imagination. With the help of friends, family, and a lot of hard work, Bill turned his childhood hobby into a tech empire that helps people all over the world.

Despite being incredibly clever, Bill wasn't a very happy student. He was, however, a

ALL IN THE FAMILY

One look at Bill's parents, and you can see that Bill inherited their drive and business savvy. Bill's dad was a respected lawyer (he even helped save Starbucks in its early days), and his mom had a career at the head of several organizations. She was also the first woman to hold multiple leadership positions at the United Way, which is a network of more than 1,800 local charities in 40 countries. Although Bill's parents didn't understand their son's love of technology, they taught Bill to dream big and helped set him up for success.

merit-badge-earning Boy Scout who read every book he could get his hands on. Bill's parents saw that he wasn't reaching his potential and decided he might do better at a private school called Lakeside School. That turned out to be a life-changing decision—one that Bill credits for the later creation of his company, Microsoft.

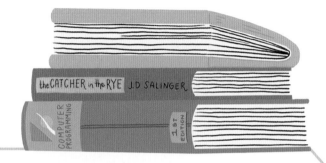

TRUE LOVE

Bill was a lot better at speaking the computer's language than he was at speaking to girls when he was young. To give him a boost, his friend Paul helped him hack into the school's scheduling system to place him in a few all-girl classes. Just being near the girls didn't help 13-year-old Bill much, though. He was still too nervous to talk to girls. But when the school caught the boys hacking, they offered Bill something even better than a date (in his eyes): unlimited computer time in exchange for boosting the computer's performance.

Lakeside gave Bill his first taste of computer programming. When an older classmate named Paul Allen saw Bill's high math scores, he asked him to join the Lakeside Programmers Group. Bill instantly fell in love with programming, but he was ahead of his time. In 1967, computers were refrigerator-size machines that cost millions of dollars, and very few people had access to them. Most people didn't know why they'd *want* access to them. Those old computers couldn't play music, connect you to your friends, or map your route—the Internet hadn't been invented yet. But Bill knew that the technology was just getting started, and he wanted in.

By the time he was 13 years old, Bill had written his first computer program—a tic-tac-toe game. Not long after, a local company called Computer Center Corporation asked him and the other Lakeside programmers to help them test their brand-new computer. It was a dream come true for Bill because it meant he could continue learning and creating. And by age 17, he had put his knowledge to good use by teaming up with Paul to form their first company. The business, a traffic-analysis program, never took off. But it taught the boys a lot about microprocessors, which would come in handy later.

Bill had been studying at Harvard for just 2 years when Paul convinced him to follow his passion for computing and to leave school for their next venture together: Microsoft. The small software company did well on its own, but a family connection helped launch it into what it is today. Bill's mom, Mary, served on the board of the United Way with the head of IBM, a company in need of an operating system for their personal computers. Mary put the tech CEO in touch with her son, and the rest was history. That contract set Bill on a path that made him a billionaire by the age of 31.

After IBM's operating system came Microsoft Windows, followed by Internet Explorer, Microsoft Office, the Xbox, and the Surface notebooks and tablets. Bill continued to dream big, but—like his mother taught him to—he shifted his focus to helping those in need. With all of the money, skill, and experience he'd earned, he knew he could change the world. In 2000, he and his wife, Melinda, officially established the Bill & Melinda Gates Foundation to do just that.

STARTING SMALL

Bill gets some of his charitable drive from his mom, who went from working as a schoolteacher to running major nonprofit organizations like the United Way. When Bill was little, his mom would ask him how much of his allowance he was planning to donate to charity. That stuck with him as he got older. Today, he's one of the biggest philanthropists in the world, donating money and resources to help make people's lives better.

Today, the foundation acts on Bill's belief in "catalytic philanthropy," which is the idea of investing in innovations that will improve life for the poorest people all over the world. Billions of dollars earned by Microsoft help ensure access to clean drinking water, to fund vaccine research to eliminate diseases, and to fight climate change. And none of that would have been possible without the big dreams of a young boy.

TIM BERNERS-LEE

COMPUTER PROGRAMMER

BORN: 1955

- Invented the World Wide Web
- Created a platform to make the World Wide Web more user-friendly as it evolves

"WE NEED DIVERSITY OF THOUGHT IN THE WORLD TO FACE THE NEW CHALLENGES."

—TIM BERNERS-LEE

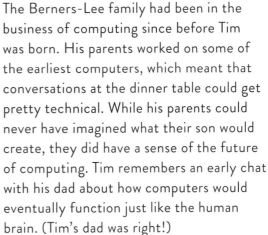

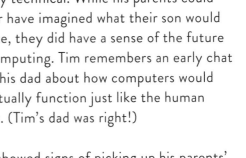

If you've searched the Internet or pulled up a web page today (and you probably have), you have Tim Berners-Lee to thank. It's incredible to think that one person could be responsible for the seemingly endless content of the World Wide Web. Although Tim is quick to point out that he didn't create something from nothing—the Internet already existed in its most basic form—he did put all the pieces together. Then he gave the code away for free and allowed the users to create the Internet we know and can't live without today. And Tim's not entirely thrilled with how things have turned out.

The Berners-Lee family had been in the business of computing since before Tim was born. His parents worked on some of the earliest computers, which meant that conversations at the dinner table could get pretty technical. While his parents could never have imagined what their son would create, they did have a sense of the future of computing. Tim remembers an early chat with his dad about how computers would eventually function just like the human brain. (Tim's dad was right!)

Tim showed signs of picking up his parents' technical skills early on. Preferring trainspotting (making note of the trains that pass by) to sports, he built a model railroad in his bedroom. But he soon realized that he was more interested in tinkering with the electronic controls than he was in the trains. When Tim got to Oxford University, his interest in electronics led him to build his own computer using an old television and a soldering iron. And then he used that computer to hack into his college's computer system (from which he was promptly banned).

Despite Tim's tech-centric upbringing, his jobs as a computer programmer never seemed to stick. That was, until he got to CERN (the European Organization for Nuclear Research) in Switzerland. There, the idea for the World Wide Web came to Tim as a solution to an annoying problem: for scientists to share information from one type of computer to another, the information had to be converted over and over again. Tim knew there had to be a better way. Many of the pieces he needed already existed, so he just had to put them together in a way that allowed people to pull up the information they needed from any computer. To Tim, it was simple. The hard part, he says, was getting people to use it.

THE POSSIBILITIES ARE LIMITLESS

Everything Tim has done since inventing the World Wide Web has been to make the Internet more useful and accessible to everyone using it. And that includes you! On his website, www.w3.org, he writes these words of encouragement to kids everywhere: "I want you to know that you too can make new programs which create new fun ways of using computers and using the Internet. I want you to realize that, if you can imagine a computer doing something, you can program a computer to do that. . . . [You're] limited only by your imagination." And according to Tim, it's a lot simpler than it seems.

Tim envisioned the World Wide Web as a haven for designers and innovators. He wanted people to feel empowered, like they had control over their little corner of the Web. And at first, they did. Computer scientists and academics got the ball rolling, and soon the World Wide Web had exploded into its first community of browsers, blogs, and shops. Then came the big corporations, like Amazon, Google, and Facebook.

Tim's not a fan of how some of these companies have used their power for their own profit at their users' expense. Data can be wielded in positive and negative ways: for example, data can be used to reach the right people,  or it can be abused to invade someone's privacy or to spread disinformation. Too many companies have been doing the latter. That's why he's decided to take back the World Wide Web, Robin Hood style. Tim established the World Wide Web Foundation in 2009 to expand Internet access, protect online privacy, champion innovation, and more. He also started hacking his own creation in order to learn how companies were using it to manipulate users.

Today, Tim is a trailblazer twice over—once for creating the Web, and again for trying to save it from itself. He's hard at work developing Solid, a platform that he hopes will help return the Web to its original mission: helping people communicate. Just like his original code, Solid is open to everyone. Turning back the clock on what we, the users, have created is going to take more work and determination than inventing the Web did. After all, there are a lot of people and companies that will fight against the changes. But Solid

A BETTER UNDERSTANDING

William Shakespeare wrote, "There is nothing either good or bad but thinking makes it so." In other words, things are only "good" or "bad" because we see them that way, or because someone uses them that way. That's how Tim thinks about the World Wide Web. At the end of the day, it's just a tool for communicating. It has the power to be good, and it has the power to be bad (just like it has the power to be both boring and interesting). It just depends on how people use it. And Tim's greatest hope is that people use it to understand each other better.

is giving Tim hope that the Web might someday exist the way he envisioned it, as a way to connect people without controlling them. All we have to do, he says, is decide that enough is enough.

BRYAN STEVENSON

HUMAN RIGHTS LAWYER

BORN: 1959

- Founded the Equal Justice Initiative, a nonprofit organization that fights to overcome racial and income inequality in the justice system
- Has helped save more than 130 wrongly accused people from death sentences

> "YOU DON'T CHANGE THE WORLD WITH THE IDEAS IN YOUR HEAD, BUT WITH THE CONVICTION IN YOUR HEART." —BRYAN STEVENSON

It's hard to imagine now, but in the future, you may look back at your life and be able to see all the moments that made you *you*. A scientist might remember their first homemade volcano, a fashion designer might think about all the clothes they made for their dolls, or a school counselor might remember how being bullied made them want to support other kids. It's never just one moment—there are little glimmers of your future hidden all over your past.

For Bryan Stevenson, those moments included listening to his grandmother tell stories about her life, going to church on Sundays, and entering the dentist's office through the back door. That might not sound like it adds up to much, but for Bryan, those are the moments that made him the accomplished legal mind and social justice warrior he is today.

Bryan was close to his grandmother, who told him stories about growing up Black in Virginia in an era when lynching was common. Black people could be lynched (hanged by a mob of people without trial) for accidentally bumping into a white person on a train or for calling a white person by their first name. In other words, they could be killed for doing things we all do every day without thinking. People of color were forced to live in fear. At the first opportunity, Bryan's grandparents fled north to Philadelphia, where they started their family.

The stories Bryan's grandmother told him helped him feel connected to his family's history, and through it, American history. Now, he's teaching others how understanding our history can help us understand how we are today, especially when it comes to our deeply flawed justice system. That includes how the United States imprisons more of its citizens than any other country in the world, and that the majority of those prisoners are poor and people of color.

Many people believe that the past is the past, but Bryan believes that we need to recognize the parts of the past that have crept into the future. Therein lies the real reason for our high incarceration rates. Ending slavery, he says, was just part of dealing with racial injustice. At the heart of the problem is white supremacy, the lie white people told themselves to justify enslaving other human beings. People of color were considered "less than" white people—less worthy, less capable, and less human.

When slavery ended, the racism and discrimination bred by that lie continued. Bryan calls it "the legacy of slavery that we haven't acknowledged."

THE FULL STORY

One of Bryan's projects has been creating the Legacy Museum in Montgomery, Alabama, where the Equal Justice Initiative is headquartered. He opened the museum around the same time that the organization unveiled their National Memorial for Peace and Justice, a memorial of 800 six-foot hanging blocks of metal inscribed with the names of lynching victims. Bryan hopes the museum, which offers an honest history of subjects like slavery, lynching, and civil rights, will help visitors better understand the full impact of these events on American life and the American criminal justice system. He believes that for change to happen, we first need to understand that it *needs* to happen.

STEVENSON

Even in Delaware, a northern state, Bryan grew up with segregation. Segregation defined which drinking fountain he could drink from, which pool he could swim in, and which entrance he could use at the dentist's office, because, more than 100 years after slavery ended, Bryan was still not considered equal to his white peers. Segregation has since ended, but discrimination persists, especially in the legal system.

That's why Bryan has devoted himself to being a champion for people who are most vulnerable. But it doesn't explain why he's also a champion for those he knows to be guilty of their crimes. That comes from growing up in the African Methodist Episcopal Church, where people were celebrated for getting up after falling down. The church taught him about faith and forgiveness. It gave him the philosophy that would compel him to fight even for inmates accused of terrible crimes: "I believe each person in our society is more than the worst thing they've ever done," he says. Bryan strives to see the whole person and the history that got them to where they are today.

To find justice for those who most desperately need it, Bryan has become an accomplished lawyer, social justice activist,

FIRSTHAND EXPERIENCE

Bryan tells the story of coming home after a long day at work and sitting in his car, listening to music, before heading in. Suddenly, a police officer was shining a flashlight in his face. When he got out of the car, the police reacted with fear and anger, one pointing a gun at him and yelling, "Move, and I'll blow your head off!" and the other slamming Bryan's body against his car. The police didn't see a Harvard graduate or a civil rights lawyer in that car. They saw a Black man, and that was enough to raise their suspicion. That's racial profiling, and it's something Bryan is working to combat.

professor, and author, as well as the founder and executive director of the Equal Justice Initiative. He's argued and won multiple cases before the Supreme Court and has saved more than 100 innocent people from death sentences. Every day, he finds new ways to teach people that knowing history can change their whole perspective.

BARACK OBAMA

PRESIDENT OF THE UNITED STATES

BORN: 1961

- 44th president of the United States and the first African American to serve in the role
- Pulled the country out of the worst economic crisis since the Great Depression

"WE ARE THE ONES WE'VE BEEN WAITING FOR. WE ARE THE CHANGE THAT WE SEEK." —PRESIDENT BARACK OBAMA

What do you dream of doing when you grow up? Does it depend on the day? You're not alone. Teenaged Barack Obama wanted to be a famous basketball player. Twenty-something Barack wanted to be a novelist. Today, Barack Obama is a Nobel Prize–winning politician and author with two terms as president of the United States under his belt. His teenaged self might not have believed it! But he just took life one step at a time, listening to his heart along the way.

It wasn't always easy for Barack to know his own heart. As the son of a Black man from Kenya and a white woman from Kansas growing up in Hawaii in the 1960s, he felt pulled in multiple directions. Add to that

a few years spent in his stepfather's native Indonesia before he moved back to live with his white grandparents in Hawaii, and you can see why Barack had a tough time feeling like he fit in anywhere. It took him decades to finally accept himself and to see his upbringing for the gift it was.

Barack's place in a diverse family spread out over multiple continents helped him see things differently than most people do. It opened his eyes to the lives and struggles of

THE NEW KID IN TOWN

Barack (or Barry, as his family called him) moved from Hawaii to Indonesia with his mom and stepfather when he was 6 years old. As a biracial kid who didn't speak the language, Barry stuck out like a sore thumb, and the other kids in his class weren't always kind. They tricked him into eating shrimp paste and hot peppers, made fun of the way he walked, and even threw him into swamp water. But Barry found ways to make the best of things until he moved back to Hawaii at age 10. He learned the language, joined local clubs, studied karate, and wrote to his grandparents about all the new things he'd seen and tried. Most importantly, he learned to stand up to his bullies without losing his cool—a skill that would come in handy down the line.

people from all different backgrounds. He had empathy (the ability to understand how others feel), but he also had hope. He knew that he could help people. After graduating from Columbia University and trying to make a career writing people's stories, Barack started to feel the pull to do more. In 1985, he took a job as a community organizer on Chicago's South Side—a poor area known for gang violence and drugs.

Organizing taught Barack how to get to the heart of a problem, to motivate people, to resolve conflicts, and to find compromises.

It also taught him to think on his feet, because things rarely worked out the way he'd planned. Motivated equally by both a desire to learn and a desire to help, Barack listened to people. He understood their needs. But organizing wasn't making the kind of impact he truly wanted to make. Barack decided that, since the law was often at the root of community issues, going to law school was the next best step he could take.

Although law school was competitive, Barack's charming personality and open-mindedness helped him make friends of his fellow students the same way he connected with people during his organizing years. Disagreements became conversations because he treated everyone with respect and genuine interest. And in his second year of law school, he became the first Black president of the *Harvard Law Review*. That's a very big honor for any

student. It meant that not only was Barack an excellent student, but he was also well respected by his peers.

After law school, Barack worked as a civil rights lawyer and a law professor before deciding he could advocate for even more people by helping to write the laws. In 1996, he was elected to the Illinois state senate. In 2004, he was elected to the U.S. Senate, becoming only the fifth Black senator in U.S. history. And just 4 years after that, in 2008, he became the first Black president of the United States.

People said that Barack didn't have enough experience to be president. But he'd spent his whole career working to help people, and that's how he spent his presidency, too. During his two terms, he helped the country bounce back from the Great Recession, ensured more people had access to affordable health care, and forged better relationships with leaders around the world. Today, he continues to help and inspire people through his writing, advocacy, and charitable work.

Barack Obama is proof that life can be even greater than you imagined. So dream big! Then just take the next best step you can take. You never know where you may end up.

SPEAKING UP

The first speech Barack ever gave was at Occidental College, when he was a 19-year-old student. Clearly nervous, he hunched over the microphone—which was positioned too low for his lanky frame—and spoke quickly. But he put his heart into his speech about the college's investments in South Africa, where apartheid meant discrimination was the law. No one knew then what Barack would become, or that speeches would become a regular part of his life. Today, he's known as a speaker with a steady pace and thoughtful pauses, but he still has the same hopeful and passionate spirit he demonstrated at 19.

SATOSHI TAJIRI

VIDEO GAME DEVELOPER

BORN: 1965

- Created Pokémon, the second most popular gaming franchise in history
- Entertained and inspired people on the autism spectrum with his success

"THE MORE I LEARNED ABOUT GAMES, THE MORE FRUSTRATED I BECAME BECAUSE THE GAMES WEREN'T VERY GOOD. . . . MY CONCLUSION WAS: LET'S MAKE OUR OWN GAMES."

—SATOSHI TAJIRI

Not every trailblazer sets out to change the world. Some just follow the spark of excitement and see where it leads. And that spark can come from anywhere. You might feel it in the words of a family member, the lesson of a teacher, or the actions of an activist. If you're anything like Satoshi Tajiri, you might even find your spark in a childhood hobby. He followed his hobby until he'd created a multimillion-dollar video-game franchise that has entertained and connected players for decades.

So, what was this magnificent hobby? Bug collecting. As a kid, Satoshi loved to explore the rice paddies, rivers, and forests around his home in Japan, discovering new and interesting creatures along the way. He was fascinated by the way insects were built, the way they walked. Insects were a mystery Satoshi wanted to uncover. At first, he brought them home to study. When that had unintended consequences (like some of the bugs eating the others), he changed his method to catch and release. But coming up with new ways to find the critters excited him most.

When Satoshi got a little older, he traded his passion for bug collecting for a devotion to video games. Together with illustrator Ken Sugimori, Satoshi created his own gaming magazine, *Game Freak*. Publishing the magazine took a lot of hard work and compromise (like moving back in with his dad), but *Game Freak* grew its readership to 10,000 people. When Satoshi and Ken realized that personal gaming systems were quickly overtaking arcade games, they turned the magazine into a development company and jumped feet first into creating games themselves.

Satoshi was just 16 years old when he first started learning how to program games. After submitting the winning concept for his first game to a contest sponsored by SEGA, he spent 3 years learning how to develop it. That experience helped him sell several games to the top gaming companies. When Satoshi first pitched Pokémon (under the name Pocket Monsters: Red and Green in Japan), Nintendo wasn't wild about the idea. But they gave their successful developer the benefit of the doubt and published the dual games anyway.

Satoshi never could have imagined the success of his creation, but he put everything he had into creating it. The monsters, you may have guessed, were inspired by the bugs Satoshi loved to collect. "Everything I did as a kid kind of rolled into one—that's what Pokémon is," he admitted. Satoshi wanted kids to enjoy that same experience of exploring in nature and discovering interesting things. He also wanted to give players a way to connect with each other.

That connection is what made Pokémon unique among games. Both the Red and Green

WHAT'S IN A NAME

In the Japanese version of Pokémon, the main character's name is Satoshi (after his creator, of course), and his rival's name is Shigeru. Satoshi named that character after legendary Japanese game developer Shigeru Myamoto, who created some of Nintendo's flagship franchises, including Super Mario, Legend of Zelda, and Donkey Kong. Satoshi sometimes refers to Shigeru as a mentor, but Shigeru is quick to give all the credit to the young developer himself. Shigeru produced the game for Nintendo, but he says that Satoshi didn't need his help developing the game—he had everything under control.

versions of the game gave players a preset collection of creatures, but neither version had all 151. To "collect them all" (the goal of the game), you needed to connect with other players physically, through Game Boy's cable, to make trades and to engage in battles. That interactive play was part of Satoshi's grand plan for the game. As soon as he saw the new Game Boy with its cable, he knew he wanted to encourage players to communicate and collaborate with each other.

Clearly, Satoshi was on to something. The original game sold millions of copies and laid the foundation for the franchise, which still releases two games in one. Today, there are nearly 1,000 Pokémon to collect. The franchise has included and inspired several versions of the games, spinoff games, trading cards, and countless toys, not to mention an anime series that ran for 900 episodes, an augmented-reality smartphone game, theme parks in Japan and Taiwan, and a live-action American movie in which actor Ryan Reynolds voiced Pikachu.

Not everyone can turn their childhood hobby into an international phenomenon, but Satoshi's success is proof that inspiration really can come

AN AUTISTIC HERO

Satoshi was diagnosed with autism as a child, which may explain his obsessions with bug collecting and video games. People on the autism spectrum can become especially engrossed in their hobbies, and a common hobby is collecting. That explains the joy Satoshi felt when collecting bugs as a kid, a joy he wanted to share with others. With Pokémon, Satoshi did that and more. Not only did he give players everywhere a new game to love, but he also gave autistic children a game that spoke directly to their needs. Although there are plenty of role models on the spectrum, Satoshi created something truly special for kids like him.

from anywhere. You just need to recognize and follow that spark of excitement when you feel it. Satoshi felt it when he collected bugs and when he started developing games, and again when he first saw the new Game Boy. By chasing that spark like a trainer after a Pikachu, Satoshi shared his joy with the world.

JOHN & HANK GREEN

AUTHORS AND ENTREPRENEURS

BORN: 1977, 1980

- Built a media company together to support learning and a sense of community
- Created the Foundation to Decrease World Suck, Inc., and Project for Awesome to raise money for charitable causes

"WE ARE THE SUPERHERO, NONE OF US INDIVIDUALLY, BUT ALL OF US TOGETHER."

—HANK GREEN

They say your siblings are your first real friends. But when you get older and busier, it can be easy to take that friendship for granted. You might not see each other as much, or even talk to each other as much. You have to make a real effort to be a part of each other's lives. That was the case for John Green (best-selling author of *The Fault in Our Stars*) and his younger brother Hank (best-selling author of *An Absolutely Remarkable Thing*). They grew up debating philosophy at the dinner table, but later they didn't seem to have those kinds of conversations anymore. All they did was text. In 2007, they decided

LIFE BEYOND MIDDLE SCHOOL

John had a tough time growing up. He was quiet and nerdy but not great at school. And he was a target for bullies. He says in one of his videos that he fantasized about making his bullies feel as scared and powerless as he felt. But now he sees what he couldn't see then—those bullies probably *did* feel scared and powerless. "They were kids, living with their own fear and pain," John says. Their behavior was about *them*. But the important thing was that he wasn't just surrounded by bullies. He was also surrounded by people who loved him, stood up for him, and helped him become the man he is today, the man who tries to show kids that there is much more to life than middle school and misery.

to change that, and that decision changed everything.

John and Hank issued themselves a challenge: spend a full year creating videos for one another on YouTube, with absolutely no texting allowed. They created their own channel (vlogbrothers) and set a schedule (alternate weekdays) and time limit (4 minutes per video). They also doled out hilarious penalties—like drinking a pureed fast-food combo meal—for missing days or going over the time limit.

Throughout the year, they talked about anything and everything, covering subjects like *Harry Potter*, climate change, earwax, bullying, and the patriarchy. They performed skits, danced, debated, and even ate toilet paper while discussing politics in Nepal. Basically, they did whatever came to mind. And they enjoyed it all so much that they decided to continue the project indefinitely. John uploads videos on Tuesdays, Hank on Fridays, and each one still clocks in under 4 minutes—or else.

By embracing their nerdiness, which they feel is just enthusiasm for a subject, John and Hank created an oddly civil little corner of the Internet. Theirs was a dedicated community of viewers who called themselves "Nerdfighters," as in, *those who fight for nerds*. And that community has made the brothers so proud by coming together to support each other, to raise money for the Greens' charitable projects, and to "fight world suck" (their favorite way of saying, "make the world a better place"). John just wishes he could have been a Nerdfighter back in his middle-school days.

LEARN AS YOU GO

The Greens' media company, Complexly, is itself a masterclass, teaching us to start before we're ready. When John and Hank started their experiment, they had no idea what they were doing. The early videos were poorly lit, poorly produced ramblings. But they kept at it, learning as they went. The brothers had patience with themselves, and they delighted in discovering new technologies and new subjects. Now, their videos are beautifully produced and are enjoyed by millions.

CRASH COURSE

Throughout the video-challenge project, which they called "Brotherhood 2.0," John and Hank grew closer. They started opening up to each other, learned new things about each other, and talked more often outside of the videos. They also started collaborating on more projects. Their 1-year experiment has morphed into a media empire that now comprises dozens of channels, projects, podcasts, and shops that focus on education, supporting independent artists, and charitable giving.

One of the Greens' most popular projects is Crash Course, an educational channel on YouTube where John, Hank, and their friends upload fun instructional videos on a variety of subjects. John tends to teach the humanities, while Hank prefers the sciences. But whether they're talking about biochemistry or they're debating who has the better Happy Dance, John and Hank infuse every video with the Nerdfighter mantra: Don't forget to be awesome (or DFTBA, for short).

OPENING UP ABOUT OCD

In John's book *Turtles All the Way Down*, he brings the issue of mental illness to the forefront through his main character's obsessive-compulsive disorder (OCD). John himself has struggled with anxiety and OCD all his life, and he feels it's important to talk about it. He wants kids to know that they can live full, happy, and amazing lives while struggling with mental health issues.

Now that the brothers share all of their projects, they don't think twice about calling the other up and sharing their ideas or venting their worries. At the end of the day, everything that they do is about connecting: with people, with ideas, and with the world. They didn't set out to start a media empire. They set out to connect with each other and, through their videos, with viewers like them. Then they built a media empire around that, with a sense of community, curiosity, and support. By choosing every project and product with genuine connection in mind, they've made the world suck a lot less for a lot of people.

"I'VE FOUND THAT SOMETIMES, OFTEN EVEN, KIDS ARE CAPABLE OF TREMENDOUS KINDNESS AND GENEROSITY." —JOHN GREEN

LIN-MANUEL MIRANDA

COMPOSER, PLAYWRIGHT, ACTOR

BORN: 1980

- Won a Pulitzer Prize, three Tony Awards, three Grammys, an Emmy, and two Olivier Awards for his boundary-breaking work
- Uses his platform to normalize diversity by telling diverse stories and hiring people of color for roles that would typically go to white actors

"YOU ARE PERFECTLY CAST IN YOUR LIFE. I CAN'T IMAGINE ANYONE BUT YOU IN THE ROLE. GO PLAY." —LIN-MANUEL MIRANDA

As Puerto Rican immigrants who prized education, Lin-Manuel's parents had high hopes for their son. They sent him to good schools and encouraged him to choose a practical and important profession: the practice of law. But, through those good schools, Lin-Manuel found his way to the theater instead, and his parents couldn't be prouder. It isn't the many, *many* awards and accolades their son has earned as an actor and composer that thrill them. It's that he, like them, made his mark on the world by taking a chance on his dreams.

Music and acting lit Lin-Manuel up from within. His mom remembers him making up songs almost as soon as he could talk. In elementary school, he was shining on stage and taping his own acts at home. He soaked up every soundtrack his parents played and every movie-musical he watched. Then his older sister, Luz, introduced him to rap and hip hop, and he fell in love with a whole new genre. By the time Lin-Manuel reached college, he had all the pieces he needed to take the world by storm.

When Lin-Manuel had to decide between teaching 7th-grade English and writing music full time, he turned to his dad. Luiz Miranda wanted to tell his son to do the rational thing. But, having given up a managing position in Puerto Rico for an uncertain future in New York, he knew firsthand that amazing things can happen when you follow your heart. He found a career and a partner he loves. And with his encouragement, Lin-Manuel would find more than a career. He would find his calling.

AN INSPIRING MELODY

Not everyone taps into their passion early on, but Lin-Manuel did. Music seemed to affect him more deeply than it affected others. Cheerful songs lifted him up while sad songs brought him to tears. And the music in Disney's animated film *The Little Mermaid* did even more than that—it inspired him to write songs of his own. (It also inspired him to name his son Sebastian after the film's calypso-singing crab.) Today, he's working on the live-action remake of that very movie alongside its original composer, Alan Menken. Talk about a dream come true!

Alongside writer Quiara Alegría Hudes, Lin-Manuel transformed *In the Heights* into an award-winning Broadway sensation (and later, a feature film) that captured all of the things he loved about immigrant-rich communities like the one he grew up in. He put their history, culture, and experiences in front of a wide audience—one that may have never seen them otherwise. And he did it with a cast full of Latino actors.

The show hadn't even finished its run when Lin-Manuel came up with his next incredible idea: a musical based on the life of American founding father Alexander Hamilton. Like *In the Heights*, *Hamilton* was no ordinary Broadway show. It mixed hip hop and rap with more traditional musical numbers, tackled modern issues, and

"FILL THE WORLD WITH MUSIC, LOVE, AND PRIDE."

—LIN-MANUEL MIRANDA

featured a cast with actors of color playing historically white roles. And it went on to earn one of the top spots in Broadway history, winning dozens of awards.

What makes Lin-Manuel's work so extraordinary goes beyond his moving plots and memorable music. He lets diversity take center stage in his projects because he understands the importance of representation (being able to see yourself reflected in positive stories and empowering roles). In addition to creating lead roles for actors of color, Lin-Manuel has given kids people to look up to who look like them. And that's something he's continued to do in his non-Broadway projects, like co-writing the music for Disney's Polynesian princess tale, *Moana*.

Lin-Manuel is quick to point out that his record-breaking musicals weren't the product of talent alone. He says, "Making words rhyme for a living is one of the great joys of my life," but it's also "a superpower I've been very conscious of developing." By meeting his dreams halfway with hard work, he's forever changed

IN THE HEIGHTS

Lin-Manuel grew up in Inwood, a mostly Latino community at the northern tip of New York City that has been home to a variety of immigrant communities over the years. But his education on the Upper East Side meant straddling two worlds—the Spanish-speaking one at home and the English-speaking one at school, where people called him "Lin" because they couldn't pronounce "Manuel." Seeing the differences between those two worlds would inspire him to create his smash hit *In the Heights*. He wrote the first version of the musical when he was just a sophomore in college.

musical theater and helped normalize representation on screen and on stage. He's also been able to create charitable programs and projects that continue his work of inspiring future generations and lifting up marginalized communities. And he's just getting started!

COLIN KAEPERNICK

QUARTERBACK AND SOCIAL ACTIVIST

BORN: 1987

- Drafted to the San Francisco 49ers, whom he led to Superbowl XLVII
- Started a social justice campaign that took the nation by storm

"OBSTACLES DON'T HAVE TO STOP YOU. IF YOU RUN INTO A WALL, DON'T TURN AROUND AND GIVE UP. FIGURE OUT HOW TO CLIMB IT, GO THROUGH IT, OR WORK AROUND IT." —COLIN KAEPERNICK

Colin Kaepernick will be the first to tell you that life doesn't always work out the way you plan. He spent his whole life planning for a career as a quarterback in the NFL. He worked hard and practiced constantly, earning a football scholarship that put him within reach of his childhood dream. And in 2011, that dream came true—Colin was drafted by the San Francisco 49ers. But soon, everything changed. At the age of 29, after playing just six seasons, Colin found himself unemployed and all but banned from playing in the league. How did he go from NFL hero to football outcast? He sat down for what he believed in.

You read that right. During an NFL pre-season game on August 26, 2016, Colin sat on the team bench while the rest of the stadium stood for the singing of the "Star-Spangled Banner," America's national anthem. It wasn't the first time Colin sat out the anthem, but it was the most widely reported. Sitting down was his silent protest against police brutality in America. Black men were being killed by police at a startling rate, and Colin had been thinking about ways to call attention to that for months. Taking a seat was just the beginning.

When asked about his protest in a later interview, Colin said, "I am not going to stand up to show pride in a flag for a country that oppresses Black people and people of color. To me, this is bigger than football and it would be selfish on my part to look the other way." He added that he would continue sitting out the anthem until he saw significant changes for people of color.

Although many people supported Colin's cause, many more were upset. They felt he was disrespecting the national anthem, the American flag, and all those who fought and died for the country they represent.

Former Green Beret Nate Boyer was one of those people. He wrote an open letter (a letter to someone that's published publicly) to Colin, telling him how the protest made him feel as a veteran.

Colin reached out to Nate and offered to meet so they could discuss each other's thoughts on the protest and what should come next. When Nate told Colin how much the anthem and flag meant to military veterans like him, Colin asked if there was a more respectful way to continue his protest. Nate had an idea. And on September 1, 2016, Nate stood with his hand over his heart next to Colin and his teammate Eric Reid as they both took a knee, a gesture that would be repeated by thousands of people. Although Colin was happy with his compromise, the NFL was not. By 2017, Colin had been forced to opt out of his contract with the 49ers. No other team would sign him.

STAYING TRUE TO YOU

Colin was born to be an athlete. Growing up, he played football, basketball, and baseball, but playing football professionally was always his dream. Due in part to his lanky frame, football scholarships didn't roll in the way Colin had hoped. He had more than a few offers to play baseball, though. To the frustration of coaches and friends, he turned them all down. Colin was smart to hold out for what he really wanted. University of Nevada offered him a football scholarship, and the rest was sports history.

KAEPERNICK 7

Colin's career as a quarterback was over, but the NFL never stopped feeling his presence. In May of 2020, a police officer knelt on a Black man's neck until he died. The man was George Floyd, and he had been suspected of a minor, nonviolent crime. People took to the streets in protest about violence

against people of color, and athletes across all sports started taking a knee just like Colin had. This time, the NFL put out a statement saying it had been wrong before and encouraging "all to speak out and peacefully protest." Suddenly, the athletes who *didn't* take a knee were the ones being criticized.

Since leaving professional sports, Colin has kept pretty busy doing the work he started when he first sat down. He gave away $1 million to 37 organizations that fight for social justice, and he founded and funded the Know Your Rights Camp. The campaign focuses on education and self-empowerment for people of color while also teaching them how to safely interact with law enforcement to defuse or avoid life-threatening situations. Colin has also released a series on Netflix called *Colin in Black & White*, which gives viewers a look at Colin in his teen years and

the moments that made him who he is today— an NFL superstar turned social activist who's just getting started. Life may not have turned out like Colin planned, but it does seem to have turned out the way it was meant to.

A COMPLICATED PERSPECTIVE

Colin was just a few weeks old when he was adopted by the Kaepernicks. As a biracial child being raised by a white family in a mostly white community, Colin had a hard time coming to terms with his racial identity. But many people in that community only saw Colin as Black. He was discriminated against by coaches, profiled by police officers, and even pigeonholed by his own friends. In order to become the strong social activist he is today, Colin had to reconcile all the different parts of himself and carve his own path forward.

BOYAN SLAT

INVENTOR AND ENVIRONMENTALIST

BORN: 1994

- Founder and CEO of The Ocean Cleanup, which aims to rid the world's oceans of plastic
- Developed and launched the world's first ocean cleanup system to make quick work of cleaning the oceans

"THERE WILL ALWAYS BE PEOPLE SAYING THINGS CAN'T BE DONE. AND HISTORY SHOWS THAT TIME AND TIME AGAIN THINGS 'COULDN'T BE DONE' AND THEY WERE DONE." —BOYAN SLAT

Boyan Slat was 16 years old when he found unlikely inspiration in a likely place. Scuba-diving with his family in the crystal-clear waters off the coast of Greece, Boyan noticed something strange: he saw more plastic bags floating around him than colorful fish. He couldn't stop thinking about it. Why was the garbage there? Why hadn't someone cleaned it up? Then he asked a better question: What would it take to clean it up?

The answer to that question started to form as Boyan did research on plastic pollution for a school project. Just 2 years

"THERE'S NO BETTER FEELING THAN HAVING AN IDEA AND SEEING IT BECOME REALITY, EMERGING IN THE PHYSICAL WORLD." —BOYAN SLAT

later, he found himself presenting his research and first attempts at ocean cleanup for a TEDx talk. At just 18 years old, Boyan claimed he knew how to use technology to rid the world's oceans of plastic. The presentation went viral. Within a year, he had received enough funding and support to leave school and start The Ocean Cleanup, a nonprofit organization dedicated to removing plastics from the ocean.

In the following years, the organization spent $7 million on creating the first ocean-cleanup system:

TEAM JENNY

TRUE DEDICATION

As much as Boyan is dedicated to his work, he'd rather skip the part where he has to be on the ocean to observe it. That's because he gets terribly seasick. And he's not just sick on the boat—he feels unwell for a week after being on the open water. Thankfully, he now leads a team of about 120 people who can monitor his invention in action and report back so that he can enjoy the ocean from dry land.

System 001, lovingly called Wilson. Creating and fine-tuning Wilson wasn't easy. Between developing the technology and adjusting for the harsh environment of the open ocean, it took years of engineering, testing, and even failure. But Boyan understands the nature of science—he knows that there can be no innovation without failure. So, he kept working and eventually released System 002, or Jenny, into the Great Pacific Garbage Patch (GPGP).

Since the 1950s, almost 9 billion tons of plastic have been produced, and 60 percent of that has ended up in landfills or in nature. Often, it finds its way to a river that feeds into an ocean, where the currents carry it out to sea. Some of it gets "caught" by the coastlines, washing up on beaches. Most of it ends up in giant patches of floating and sinking debris when it hits one of five massive, spiraling currents, called *gyres*.

One of those gyres is home to the GPGP, which is twice the size of Texas and, because of the spiraling currents, isn't going anywhere. The longer plastics linger in the water, the more they break down into dangerous microplastics that can pollute waters and kill sea life. The plastic also makes its way into the food chain as creatures consume it—the same creatures that often end up on our dinner plates. That's why Boyan is sending Jenny in to clean it up.

Boyan designed his systems to use the same currents that were catching and moving the garbage to begin with. He ensures that sea life doesn't get tangled up with the trash by using a slow-moving curtain instead of a fast-gathering net. And that curtain mimics the way a coastline collects garbage. "Coastlines are very effective ways of catching plastic," he says. "But the thing is, in those vast ocean garbage patches, there's simply no coastlines to catch any plastic. So we built our own artificial coastline." But he keeps working and improving on each system—first Wilson, then Jenny, and next, System 003, which will be the model for a fleet of vessels ready to clean up all of the world's oceans.

Boyan knows that there are a lot of ways to tackle this problem, like changing the way we use plastic, cleaning up the beaches, and keeping more garbage from entering the ocean through rivers. And he thinks we should do all of it. That's why he's developed another piece of technology: The Interceptor, a solar-powered cleanup vessel made specifically for rivers. His research team determined that 1,000 rivers were responsible for 80 percent of the pollution in the oceans, and he plans to clean them all up in just 5 years.

Cleaning up the oceans and rivers won't put a stop to plastic pollution—we can only do that by drastically reducing the amount of plastic and waste we create. But it's a brilliant start. And Boyan's pretty sure that seeing all of the trash his vessels collect and having clean oceans for the first time in a generation will be motivation enough. If nothing else, it's motivation to keep trying!

CLEANING UP AT HOME

Take a look around the room. How many pieces of plastic can you count? Can you imagine the world without those things? Probably not. That's why it's easy to imagine that plastic was always an essential part of life. But just 60 years ago, that wasn't the case. Glass and aluminum were far more common. They were also far more eco-friendly at the time, but people liked the convenience of plastic. Today, we can find that same convenience in reusable bags, biodegradable wrapping, recycled materials, and yes, glass and aluminum packaging. By buying eco-friendly products, we can help keep harmful garbage out of the oceans so that Boyan doesn't have to clean up after us.

THE OCEAN CLEANUP

INTERCEPTOR
003

DAVID HOGG

SOCIAL ACTIVIST AND ORGANIZER

BORN: 2000

- Became a leading gun-control advocate after surviving a school shooting
- Cofounded March for Our Lives and helped organize one of the biggest marches in U.S. history

"LEADERSHIP IS MOST IMPORTANT WHEN IT'S THE HARDEST." –DAVID HOGG

David Hogg crouched in a dark classroom, listening to the sound of gunshots. He quickly realized this was not an active-shooter *drill*. This was an *active shooter*, in *his* high school. He did the only thing he could do in that moment: he turned on his phone's camera and started recording. Those moments when he narrated what was happening at Marjory Stoneman Douglas High would turn out to be just the beginning in a courageous fight against gun violence.

David lost 17 of his classmates that Valentine's Day in 2018. Before the shooting, he was applying to colleges and dreaming about becoming a journalist or an aerospace engineer. After the shooting, all he could do was focus on making sure no one else had to go through the fear and loss that his community of Parkland, Florida, had just experienced. And that meant becoming one of the faces of the tragedy, giving speeches and interviews that would be splashed all over the news.

Although David didn't choose the high-profile activist life, he embraced it. When he got home, he offered his recording to the *Sun Sentinel*, the newspaper he interned for. Then, despite his dad's concern, he biked back to school to give an interview to the first producer he could find. For a high school student who had just been through a life-changing ordeal, David was calm throughout his television interview. He even seized the last few seconds to plead with the audience not to quickly forget this tragedy but instead to face the issue of gun violence head-on. The host ended the interview, but David was far from finished.

In the coming days, David and his friends shared an important message with the world: They weren't scared. They were angry. They saw what happened as a failure of the U.S. government to protect people from gun violence. In their view, not enough people had been angry about school shootings until now. People were devastated but also hopeless, like nothing could be done. David and his classmates didn't accept that. Instead, they demanded change. And by telling their stories and talking about how the shooting affected them, they drew national attention to the issue.

With the spotlight suddenly shining brightly on them, David and several other students worked to hold onto that attention. They organized peaceful protests and marches, like the March for Our Lives (MFOL) on March 24, 2018. David was one of the creators of both that event—which was one of the largest demonstrations in U.S. history—and the organization it launched by the same name. Their mission: "To harness the power of young people across the country to fight for sensible gun violence prevention policies that save lives."

OVERCOMING DYSLEXIA

Growing up, David struggled with dyslexia (a learning disorder that makes it hard to read and write). Because he didn't learn to read until he was 9 years old, he worked doubly hard on his speaking skills. He even joined the debate team to prove to himself and his classmates that his dyslexia didn't slow him down. Joining debate meant learning about complex issues, choosing a side, and defending it—a process that takes critical-thinking and communication skills. One of the issues David debated was gun control, and he had to argue both sides. Little did he know how his time on the team would prepare him for his future as an activist. Today, David is an eloquent speaker and a proud member of Harvard's class of 2023.

David's quick to point out that he's not against responsible gun ownership—his father is a former FBI agent and owns guns. He's against the kind of lax regulations that allowed a mentally unstable young man to buy a gun and turn it on his fellow students. He and the other members of MFOL are calling for not only sensible gun control laws but also ways to address the root causes of gun violence, like systems that ignore or even encourage poverty, mental health issues, and feelings of supremacy.

Not everyone is a fan of David's work—he's faced harassment and threats over the years. But what concerns him more is apathy (people not caring enough to get involved). In addition to demanding action on gun violence, David is hard at work encouraging young people to take an

ELEVATING MINORITY VOICES

One of the reasons David felt it was so important for Parkland survivors to raise the alarm on gun violence was that the school's mostly white victims attracted more media attention than many victims of color do. Yet, more often than not, it's people of color who are most deeply affected by gun violence. David once said, "If our school had been in a different zip code, we wouldn't have got the same coverage." He makes sure to acknowledge that privilege and use it to lift up the voices of those who are most affected by gun violence.

interest in government. He educates crowds and Twitter followers about the importance of understanding the issues, of voting, and of fighting for a better future for themselves and those who come after them. He has dreams of revamping school lessons and maybe even running for Congress to continue that work. One thing's for sure: years after demanding change on the lawn of Marjory Stoneman Douglas High, David Hogg is still far from finished.

ABOUT THE AUTHOR & ILLUSTRATOR

JENNIFER CALVERT is a writer, editor, and all-around book-loving nerd. She's the author of *Science Superstars: 30 Brilliant Women Who Changed the World* and *Teen Trailblazers: 30 Fearless Girls Who Changed the World Before They Were 20*. When she's not highlighting the accomplishments of incredible people, you'll find her curled up with a soft cat and a hardcover.

VESNA ASANOVIC is an illustrator living in Toronto. She holds a bachelor's degree from Ontario College of Art and Design. She works primarily digitally with a particular interest in bright, bold colors and graphic shapes. In her free time you can find Vesna drawing in her sketchbook on a sunny patio.

IF YOU LIKE THIS BOOK, YOU MIGHT ALSO LIKE:

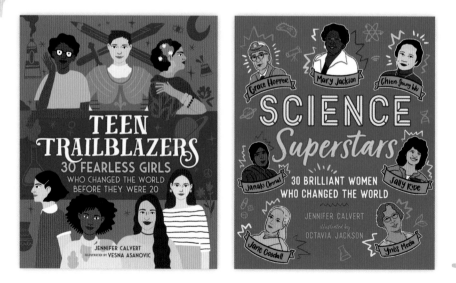